D0943775

Twelve-Tone Tonality

George Perle

TWELVE-TONE TONALITY

CEDAR CREST COLLEGE LIBRARY
ALLENTOWN, PA. 18104

UNIVERSITY OF CALIFORNIA PRESS
Berkeley · Los Angeles · London

790816

University of California Press
Berkeley and Los Angeles, California

University of California Press, Ltd.
London, England

Copyright © 1977 by
The Regents of the University of California

ISBN 0-520-03387-6
Library of Congress Catalog Card Number: 76-50258
Printed in the United States of America

1 2 3 4 5 6 7 8 9

To Maurice Rogalin

Contents

*Basic definitions listed in the index appear in boldface in the text.

Preface

The theory set forth in the following pages had its inception, almost forty years ago, in a misunderstanding. Uninstructed as I was in Schoenberg's "twelve-tone system," I correctly assumed that the adjacencies comprised in the forty-eight different forms of a given twelve-tone row were a collective statement of the relations assigned to each element of the semitonal scale, but it did not occur to me that the tone row in itself was to be construed as a unitary linear structure. My first attempt at what I took to be twelve-tone composition was based on the following P and I row forms:

$$b \quad c \quad d \quad f \quad a \quad a^\flat \quad g \quad f^\sharp \quad d^\sharp \quad e \quad b^\flat \quad c^\sharp \quad (b$$

$$b \quad b^\flat \quad a^\flat \quad f \quad c^\sharp \quad d \quad d^\sharp \quad e \quad g \quad f^\sharp \quad c \quad a \quad (b$$

From these I derived a collection of adjacency relations by pairing three-note segments that shared the same pivotal pitch class, as in the following array, in which the horizontally stated segments are taken from P and the intersecting vertically stated segments from I:

$$
\begin{array}{llllll}
f^\sharp & f & c^\sharp & d & d^\sharp & a^\flat \\
b \;\; c \;\; d & b^\flat \;\; c^\sharp \;\; b & c \;\; d \;\; f & f^\sharp \;\; d^\sharp \;\; e & d^\sharp \;\; e \;\; b^\flat & d \;\; f \;\; a \\
a & d & d^\sharp & e & g & c^\sharp \\
\end{array}
$$

$$
\begin{array}{llllll}
g & e & b^\flat & c & b & a \\
g \;\; f^\sharp \;\; d^\sharp & a^\flat \;\; g \;\; f^\sharp & a \;\; a^\flat \;\; g & f \;\; a \;\; a^\flat & e \;\; b^\flat \;\; c^\sharp & c^\sharp \;\; b \;\; c \\
c & f^\sharp & f & b & a^\flat & b^\flat \\
\end{array}
$$

In effect, the distinction between retrograde-related row forms was eliminated and any note was free to move to either of its neighbors in either of two inversionally complementary forms.

I soon realized, of course, that I had misunderstood Schoenberg's concept of the tone row. In Schoenberg's system pitch classes are not, in general, assumed to be points of intersection between different forms of the row. For Schoenberg the row, though "invented to substitute for some of the unifying and formative advantages of scale and tonality," also "functions in the manner of a motive."* I found this motivic concept uncongenial, but I also found that my own interpretation of the row as a precompositional collection of neighbor-note configurations could not provide a meaningful basis for twelve-tone composition, except where

*Style and Idea (New York: St. Martin's Press, 1975), p. 219.

it was applied to a very special type of set structure. Where such configurations were derived from the general set they were too haphazard and too fortuitous to be useful.

This special type of tone row is the "cyclic set," in which the notes that are neighbors to each element always form the same interval. Let us assume, for example, that the recurrent interval is the "perfect fifth." A tone row whose alternate elements unfold along diverging cycles of "perfect fifths" will give us, as neighbor notes to each pitch class, a different transposition of this interval. It was only many years later that I came to realize that the two concepts joined in such a set—the interval cycle and inversional complementation—had both played an enormously significant role in the evolution of post-diatonic music long before I came upon the cyclic set as a solution to certain immediate theoretical and practical problems. (The reader is referred to my article, "Berg's Master Array of the Interval Cycles," *The Musical Quarterly*, LXIII (1977), pp. 1ff.)

Suppose now we replace our earlier pair of P and I row forms by P and I forms of the cyclic set. For example:

$c)$ *c   g   f   d   b♭   a   d♯   e   g♯   b   c♯   f♯   (f♯   c♯*...

$d)$ *d   g   a   c   e   f   b   b♭   f♯   d♯   c♯   g♯   (g♯   c♯*...

The following array of adjacency relations is produced:

```
      a            g♯          g           f♯           f            e
 c  c   g       b c♯ f♯     b♭ d  f     a  d♯ e      g♯ e  d♯      g  f  d
      e            d♯          d           c♯           c            b

      d♯           d           c♯          c            b            b♭
f♯ f♯ c♯        f g  c      e g♯ b      d♯ a  b♭     d  b♭ a      c♯ b  g♯
      b♭           a           g♯          g            f♯           f
```

What I called "the twelve-tone modal system" was based on these principles of set structure and set association. It governed much of my own work as a composer between 1940 and 1969, as a personal solution to what everyone has recognized as the most problematical aspect of twelve-tone composition, its harmonic organization. (See the second edition [1968] of my book, *Serial Composition and Atonality*, pp. 104–113.)

In the summer of 1969 Paul Lansky made certain suggestions that led to a long and intensive period of collaboration. The resulting radical expansion of the original theory was described in an interim report in the third edition (1971) of *Serial Composition and Atonality*. This has since been superseded on Mr. Lansky's part by his doctoral dissertation, *Affine Music* (Princeton University, 1973), and on my part by the monograph which follows.

The preceding letter-notation array is given in conventional pitch notation in examples 15 and 16, with the ordering of the twelve "chords" changed so that they unfold along inversionally related cycles of "perfect fifths" rather than semitones. If we substitute the integers 0, 1, 2, . . . for the conventional letter or pitch notation, we can define the respect in which all twelve chords are identical. These and only these chords are generated when pitch-class n is combined with pitch-classes $9\text{-}n$, $0\text{-}n$, $4\text{-}n$, $7\text{-}n$.** I hope that the use of number notation to define relations among pitches and pitch classes will not cause the reader to misconstrue the nature of these relations. The preceding array becomes neither more nor less "mathematical" when it is converted to the following notation:

	9			8			7			6			5			4	
0	0	7	11	1	6	10	2	5	9	3	4	8	4	3	7	5	2
	4			3			2			1			0			11	

	3			2			1			0			11			10	
6	6	1	5	7	0	4	8	11	3	9	10	2	10	9	1	11	8
	10			9			8			7			6			5	

The musically competent but mathematically incompetent reader will easily learn to respond with the appropriate aural imagery to pitch-class number notation. The reader in whom such a response is not induced by letter or pitch notation has a much more serious problem, regardless of his mathematical competence.

ACKNOWLEDGMENTS

Special thanks are due to Robby Merkin for his careful reading of the manuscript and proofs and for his many helpful suggestions.

For permission to reprint copyrighted material, acknowledgment is gratefully made to the following:
Belmont Music Publishers, Los Angeles, Ca.
Boelke-Bomart, Inc., Hillsdale, N.Y.
Galaxy Music Corporation, New York, N.Y.
Margun Music Inc., Newton Center, Mass.
Theodore Presser Company, Bryn Mawr, Pa.
Universal Edition, A.G., Vienna.
The Musical Quarterly, New York, N.Y.
   1976   G.P.

**When n is larger than the integer from which it is subtracted add 12 (for the octave) to the latter.

1. Introduction

Like other scales, the semitonal scale of atonal and twelve-tone music defines a pitch-class domain. But, unlike the others, the semitonal scale comprises all twelve pitch classes and makes no functional distinctions among them. And where each cyclic permutation of a pentatonic or diatonic scale represents another "mode," by unfolding a different permutation of the series of intervals that separate adjacent degrees of the scale, the interval pattern of the scale of atonal and twelve-tone music is always the same. A change in the octave boundary of the semitonal scale is equivalent to a transposition, and neither is a meaningful operation.

Around 1920 Arnold Schoenberg and Josef Matthias Hauer independently arrived at the concept of the twelve-tone set as a means of conferring referential implications upon twelve-tone pitch-class collections. **In Hauer's system the twelve pitch classes of the semitonal scale are divided into mutually exclusive sub-collections of unordered content. Each transposition of a given partitioning is a different representation of the same "trope."**[1] **In Schoenberg's system a specific ordering is assigned to the twelve pitch classes. Each transposition of a given ordering is a different representation of the same "row."** In Hauer's system the absolute pitch-class content of each segment of the set is revised under transposition, but its relative content remains the same; in Schoenberg's the order of pitch classes is revised under transposition, but the series of intervals unfolded by the set remains the same. **For any type of scale or set, transpositional equivalence has the same meaning: two scales or sets are equivalent by transposition (i.e., they are different representations of the same scale, the same trope, or the same row) where the same difference is found between corresponding pitch classes in a one-to-one alignment of both.** For example, such an alignment of the initial set of Schoenberg's Fourth Quartet with the set in the opening bars of the third movement, P_2 and P_0 respectively,[2] shows a

---

1. The only tropes that Hauer investigated systematically are those that divide the twelve pitch classes into two hexachords. The principle of partitioning as a means of differentiating collections of the twelve pitch classes is applicable, of course, to any other type of segmentation.

2. **The subscript shows the pitch-class number of the initial element of the given form of the row, where that form is P or I, with 0 always standing for c, 1 always standing for $c\sharp$ or $d\flat$, and so on.** For R and RI the subscript refers to the pitch-class number of the final element of the given form. **Where a given set is transposed, the interval of transposition is shown by a "T number," which names the repeated difference found by subtracting each pitch-class number of the given set from the corresponding pitch-class number of the transposed set.** In the present example P_0 is a T(10) transposition of P_2.

constant difference of 10 if we subtract each pitch-class number of P_2 from the identically ordered pitch-class number of P_0:

P_0: 0 11 7   8 3 1 2 10 6 5 4   9

P_2: 2   1 9 10 5 3 4   0 8 7 6 11

The assumption of a hexachordal segmentation of each set, with no implication as to the respective order of the two hexachords or the respective order of pitch classes within each hexachord, converts Schoenberg's row into one of Hauer's tropes. The given row is only one of 518,400 (=6!×6!) different rows that may be derived from the same trope. The ordering assigned to pitch classes within each segment of the following transpositionally related forms of this trope is arbitrary:

(P_0): 0 1 3 7   8 11 / 6   9 10 2 4 5

(P_2): 2 3 5 9 10   1 / 8 11   0 4 6 7

In Schoenberg's system inversionally related sets are also assumed to be different representations of the same row. Where transpositionally related sets show the same difference for every pair of corresponding pitch classes, inversionally related sets show the same sum. For the initial pair of P and I sets in the Fourth Quartet this "sum of complementation" is 9:

P_2: 2 1 9 10 5 3 4 0 8 7 6 11

I_7: 7 8 0 11 4 6 5 9 1 2 3 10

The trope representations of these sets may be respectively illustrated as follows:

(P_2): 2 3 5 9 10   1 / 8 11 0 4 6 7

(I_7): 7 6 4 0 11   8 / 1 10 9 5 3 2

The two tropes are identical, since their hexachordal content is the same. Any other transposition of I relative to the original transposition of P would have produced hexachords of non-identical but transpositionally equivalent content. For example:

(P_2): 2 3 5 9 10   1 / 8 11   0 4 6 7

(I_9): 9 8 6 2   1 10 / 3   0 11 7 5 4

The recurrent sum in this case is 11. A retrograde representation of either set produces a transposition of the other. For example:

(P_2): 2 3 5   9 10 1 /   8 11 0 4 6 7

(RI_9) = (P_4): 4 5 7 11   0 3 / 10   1 2 6 8 9

In Hauer's system inversionally related sets which do *not* share the same or transpositionally equivalent hexachordal content are classified as independent tropes. However, since inversional complementation, like transposition, is an operation that affects only the pitch-class number of each element of the set, the concept of inversional equivalence is as applicable to Hauer's tropes as it is to Schoenberg's rows.

It is not, however, applicable to the traditional diatonic scales and modes. While it is true, for example, that the pitch classes of the C major scale and the pitch classes of the E phrygian scale complement one another at sum 4,

$$c \quad d \quad e \quad f \quad g \quad a \quad b \quad c$$

$$e \quad d \quad c \quad b \quad a \quad g \quad f \quad e$$

in order to show that the two scales are inversionally related we must also establish, among other things, that the lower fifth and super-tonic degrees of the second scale are respectively equivalent in function to the dominant and leading tone of the first. Similarly, as pitch-class collections major triads are equivalent by inversion to minor triads, but unless we can show that what we ordinarily call the "fifth" of a minor triad is really its "root," and vice versa, the observation is trivial. The replacement of a collection of functionally differentiated notes whose scalar ordering produces a series of whole steps and half steps, by a collection of functionally undifferentiated notes whose scalar ordering produces a series of half steps only, completely transforms the meaning of inversion, which now becomes a precompositional means of symmetrically partitioning the tone material. The inversion of themes and motives in diatonic music occurs in a prior harmonic context whose functional relations are not invertible, and it is rarely literal, since it is not measured in terms of a single unit but rather in terms of diatonic intervals that differ in dimension as well as in harmonic implication. Inversional complementation in post-diatonic music, on the other hand, generates the harmonic context and is, by definition, literal.[3]

In Schoenberg's twelve-tone system the concept of inversional equivalence is explicitly formulated, for the first time, as one of the axiomatic bases of a musical language, analogous to the traditional concept of transpositional equivalence in its significance as a foundational premise.[4]

3. The fact that Schoenberg himself, in his theoretical writings, frequently equates inversional complementation and the other basic transformation procedures of twelve-tone music with thematic operations in diatonic music is beside the point. He did not, and could not, equate them as a *composer* of twelve-tone music. Cf. my review of *Style and Idea* in *The Musical Quarterly,* LXII/3 (1976), p. 440.

4. Obviously, inversional equivalence does not imply that it is immaterial whether we play Schoenberg's Opus 33a as he wrote it or upside down. According to Edward T. Cone ("Beyond Analysis," *Perspectives of New Music,* VI/1 (1967), 33ff.), the conclusion that it *is* immaterial "might be drawn from reading much, and perhaps most, accepted twelve-tone

The same concept of inversional equivalence is implied in much of the non-serial atonal music that precedes the twelve-tone system and in much of the work of one composer who was outside of Schoenberg's circle, Béla Bartók.[5]

As we have seen, transposition and inversion are basic operations that are equally applicable to either type of twelve-tone set, the trope or the row. The remaining axiomatic transformation procedure of Schoenberg's system, retrogression, is applicable only to the row, since it affects the order numbers of the elements of the set. The retrograde statement of a P or I set at any transposition is assumed to be another representation of the same row, and may be defined in terms of the complementation of the order numbers of the given P or I set.[6] Order-number complementation has no relevance to the subject of the present study.

---

analysis today." The inadequacy of analysis that carries such an implication is self-evident. I agree with Mr. Cone, that (his emphasis) *"concrete musical values depend on absolute decisions"* and that such decisions are "independent of purely analytical considerations and unsusceptible of purely analytical justification." Elsewhere in the same article he points to register in tonal music as one "source of associative values," and asserts that such values "presuppose absolute decisions;" yet nowhere does he take traditional theory to task for its failure to show the limits of the axiom of octave equivalence. Why should he not draw the conclusion, from any harmony book, that in its author's view it is immaterial whether we play Chopin's C minor Prelude as he wrote it or an octave higher?

In my discussion of Opus 33a in *Serial Composition and Atonality* I described the way in which "the essential shape of the whole movement is microcosmically contained in the melodic arch of the first two bars." Is it because I failed to point out that an inverted melodic arch would not have the same expressive effect, and that therefore the composition as a whole can *not* be inverted, in spite of the axiom of inversional equivalence, that Mr. Cone includes me among the authors whom he takes to task? Such a statement would be as trivial and superfluous, though all-important, as the considerations that might be offered to explain why the Chopin composition should not be played in the higher octave.

The reason for Mr. Cone's inconsistent attitude lies in his concern, which I share, that "a great deal of current writing on music seems to imply that nothing about composition, or nothing important about composition, is beyond analysis." I hasten to disclaim such an implication in my own writings on music, but I also disclaim any intention to discuss things that are "beyond analysis" in writings about music that are entirely concerned with analysis.

5. Studies of inversional complementation in post-diatonic non-serial music include Perle, "Symmetrical Formations in the String Quartets of Béla Bartók," *Music Review,* XVI (1955), pp. 300ff.; Leo Treitler, "Harmonic Procedures in the Fourth Quartet of Béla Bartók," *Journal of Music Theory,* III (1959), pp. 292ff.; Elliott Antokoletz, *Principles of Pitch Organization in Bartók's Fourth String Quartet,* Ph.D. dissertation, City University of New York, 1975; Bruce Archibald, "Some Thoughts on Symmetry in Early Webern; Op. 5, No. 2," *Perspectives of New Music,* X/2 (1972), pp. 159ff.; Perle, *Serial Composition and Atonality,* Chapter II (on the first movement of the Serenade, Opus 24, by Schoenberg); and Perle, "Berg's Master Array of the Interval Cycles," cited above, p. ii. (Several excerpts from the last are incorporated in the following pages, with the kind permission of Christopher Hatch, former editor of *The Musical Quarterly.*)

6. Milton Babbitt, "Twelve-Tone Invariants as Compositional Determinants," *The Musical Quarterly,* XLVI (1960), pp. 246ff. This issue has been reprinted as *Problems of Modern Music* (New York: Norton, 1960).

2. Inversionally Complementary Cycles

An ordered set is one of 479,001,600 permutations of the semitonal scale. By transposition or inversion each element of a given ordered set is convertible into an element of a second ordered set, such that respective elements of the two sets, identical as to order number, are different as to pitch-class number by a constant interval number or a constant sum. The pitch-class relations between *any* pair of such ordered sets is reducible to the pitch-class relations between two representations of the semitonal scale. For example, the relations between corresponding pitch classes of the P_2 and P_0 sets illustrated above, or of any other pair of sets of which the second is a $T(10)$ transposition of the first, are all expressed in the following alignment of parallel semitonal scales:

$$0 \quad 1 \quad 2 \quad 3 \quad 4 \quad 5 \quad 6 \quad 7 \quad 8 \quad 9 \quad 10 \quad 11 \quad (0$$

$$2 \quad 3 \quad 4 \quad 5 \quad 6 \quad 7 \quad 8 \quad 9 \quad 10 \quad 11 \quad 0 \quad 1 \quad (2$$

Similarly, the pitch-class relations between any pair of inversionally related sets is reducible to the pitch-class relations between two inversionally related representations of the semitonal scale. For example, the relations between corresponding pitch classes of the P_2 and I_7 sets illustrated above, or of any other pair of sets of which one is the inversion of the other at sum of complementation 9, are all expressed in the following alignment of inversionally related semitonal scales:

$$4 \quad 5 \quad 6 \quad 7 \quad 8 \quad 9 \quad 10 \quad 11 \quad 0 \quad 1 \quad 2 \quad 3 \quad (4$$

$$5 \quad 4 \quad 3 \quad 2 \quad 1 \quad 0 \quad 11 \quad 10 \quad 9 \quad 8 \quad 7 \quad 6 \quad (5$$

The maintenance of a single sum of complementation among *different* pairs of inversionally related forms of the row is a principle that is found in several of Webern's compositions. The following diagram shows the succession of row forms employed in the first movement of the Quartet, Opus 22, for violin, clarinet, tenor saxophone, and piano:

P_1	P_7	P_1	P_{10}	P_{11}	R_0	P_0	R_1	P_7	P_1	R_1
I_{11}	I_5	I_{11}	I_2	I_1	RI_0	I_0	RI_{11}	I_5	I_{11}	RI_{11}
		$(I_1 \quad I_7)$						$(I_1 \quad I_7)$		

With the exception of the forms shown in parentheses, each form is paired with an inversionally related form, the respective pitch levels of the two always being such as to produce the inversional relations represented in the following alignment of opposite semitonal scales:

$$0 \quad 1 \quad 2 \quad 3 \quad 4 \quad 5 \quad 6 \quad 7 \quad 8 \quad 9 \quad 10 \quad 11 \quad (0$$

$$0 \quad 11 \quad 10 \quad 9 \quad 8 \quad 7 \quad 6 \quad 5 \quad 4 \quad 3 \quad 2 \quad 1 \quad (0$$

This series of vertical dyads is permuted as follows in the initial pair of row forms:

$$P_1: \quad 1 \quad 10 \quad 9 \quad 0 \quad 11 \quad 3 \quad 4 \quad 5 \quad 6 \quad 8 \quad 2 \quad 7$$

$$I_{11}: \quad 11 \quad 2 \quad 3 \quad 0 \quad 1 \quad 9 \quad 8 \quad 7 \quad 6 \quad 4 \quad 10 \quad 5$$

Every other pair of row forms in the movement is another permutation of the same collection of dyads. **We will call such inversionally related dyads "P/I" dyads.**

The Variations for piano, Opus 27, and the Symphony, Opus 21, are based on different rows, but the second movement of the former and the first movement, bars 1–26 and 43–66, of the latter maintain the same complementary relations between pairs of pitch classes:

$$9 \quad 10 \quad 11 \quad 0 \quad 1 \quad 2 \quad 3 \quad 4 \quad 5 \quad 6 \quad 7 \quad 8 \quad (9$$

$$9 \quad 8 \quad 7 \quad 6 \quad 5 \quad 4 \quad 3 \quad 2 \quad 1 \quad 0 \quad 11 \quad 10 \quad (9$$

If we apply the same point of reference, c=0, in assigning T-nos. to both rows, the paired row forms that generate these relations will be named P_8 I_{10}, P_3 I_3, P_{10} I_8, and P_1 I_5 for the Variations and P_9 I_9, P_1 I_5, P_6 I_0, and P_2 I_4 for the Symphony. **In every instance the sum of the paired T-nos. is 6 (=18), that is, twice the pitch-class number of *a* (9) or *d$\sharp$* (3), the dual axis of symmetry (i.e., the points of intersection of the inversionally related cycles).**

The same principle of row-form association governs a large section of Act II, Sc. 1, of Berg's *Lulu*.[7] The priority of sums of complementation 9 and 7 as the bases of pitch relations, over the ordering imposed by a given set structure, is explicitly asserted in that the same collections of P/I dyads are derived from different rows. The *Lied der Lulu*, for example, commences with P_0 and I_7 of the basic row of the opera:

$$0 \quad 4 \quad 5 \quad 2 \quad 7 \quad 9 \quad 6 \quad 8 \quad 11 \quad 10 \quad 3 \quad 1$$

$$7 \quad 3 \quad 2 \quad 5 \quad 0 \quad 10 \quad 1 \quad 11 \quad 8 \quad 9 \quad 4 \quad 6$$

The same P/I dyads are derived from the P_1 and I_6 forms of Dr. Schoen's row at the beginning of the third strophe of his aria:

7. See Douglas Jarman, "Dr. Schön's Five-Strophe Aria; Some Notes on Tonality and Pitch Association in Berg's *Lulu*," *Perspectives of New Music*, VIII/2 (1970), pp. 23ff.

1   6   10   11   5   8   7   0   2   3   9   4

6   1   9   8   2   11   0   7   5   4   10   3

In Schoenberg's "combinatorial" pieces[8] the sum of complementation determines the respective segmental content of the row. In the Piano Piece, Opus 33a, for example, each dyad of sum 1,

$$0/1, 2/11, 3/10, 4/9, 5/8, 6/7$$

is divided between the two hexachords of the principal P set:

P_{10}:   10   5   0   11   9   6 / 1   3   7   8   2   4

The principal I set is complementary to P_{10} at sum 1. It therefore reorders the pitch-class content of the respective hexachords of P_{10}:

I_3:   3   8   1   2   4   7 / 0   10   6   5   11   9

A different partitioning of the same P/I dyads establishes a "combinatorial" relation between P_4 and I_9 at the beginning of the second movement of the Violin Concerto. so that, again, each pair of P and I hexachords comprises all twelve pitch classes:

P_4:   4   5   10   6   11   1 / 7   8   2   3   9   0

I_9:   9   8   3   7   2   0 / 6   5   11   10   4   1

Let us call the ascending form of the semitonal scale a "P cycle" and the descending form an "I cycle." The intervals generated by the aligned cycles may be represented by subtracting each member of the I cycle from the complementary member of the P cycle. Each interval will appear at two pitch levels, separated by the tritone. Where the sum of complementary pitch-class numbers is even, the interval numbers will be even, and where that sum is odd the interval numbers will be odd. The paired P and I cycles intersecting at *a* and *d*♯, for example, generate a series of even intervals whose transpositional level is indicated by the sum of complementation, 6, or 18.

P/I Dyads of Sum 6

P Cycle:	9	10	11	0	1	2	3	4	5	6	7	8	(9
I Cycle:	9	8	7	6	5	4	3	2	1	0	11	10	(9
Intervals:	0	2	4	6	8	10	0	2	4	6	8	10	(0

Any realignment of the semitonal cycles that displaces either by an even number of semitones relative to the other will generate the same collection of interval classes at a new pitch level. The principal "tonality"

8. See Perle, *Serial Composition and Atonality*, pp. 96ff. All page references, unless otherwise indicated, are to the 4th edition.

of Webern's Quartet, Opus 22, for example, is represented when P and I cycles are aligned so that they intersect at pitch-class 0 and at pitch-class 6:

P/I Dyads of Sum 0

P Cycle:	9	10	11	0	1	2	3	4	5	6	7	8	(9
I Cycle:	3	2	1	0	11	10	9	8	7	6	5	4	(3
Intervals:	6	8	10	0	2	4	6	8	10	0	2	4	(6

Where P and I cycles are aligned to form P/I dyads of an odd sum, they will intersect at intervals 11 and 1. For example:

P/I Dyads of Sum 9

P Cycle:	9	10	11	0	1	2	3	4	5	6	7	8	(9
I Cycle:	0	11	10	9	8	7	6	5	4	3	2	1	(0
Intervals:	9	11	1	3	5	7	9	11	1	3	5	7	(9

The dual axis of symmetry here is *a♯/b* and *e/f*. The pairing of inversionally complementary hexachords of mutually exclusive pitch-class content, as in those of Schoenberg's works that are based on combinatorial rows, will always require an odd sum of complementation, since otherwise there will be pitch-class duplication where the cycles intersect. Obviously, where a pitch class is its own complement the P/I dyad cannot be partitioned between the two segments of a single row form. The principal P and I row forms of Schoenberg's Fourth Quartet, for example, permute the above series of P/I dyads of sum 9 as follows:

P_2:	2	1	9	10	5	3	/	4	0	8	7	6	11
I_7:	7	8	0	11	4	6	/	5	9	1	2	3	10
Intervals:	7	5	9	11	1	9		11	3	7	5	3	1

In the development section of Opus 33a the principal row forms, P_{10} and I_3, are first transposed by T(2) and then by T(7). Any change in the pitch level of a given row form will change the implied sum of complementation by twice the difference in semitones between the two pitch levels. The original sum of complementation, 1,

P_{10}:	10	5	0	11	9	6	/	1	3	7	8	2	4
I_3:	3	8	1	2	4	7	/	0	10	6	5	11	9
Intervals:	7	9	11	9	5	11		1	5	1	3	3	7

is thus replaced by 5,

P_0:	0	7	2	1	11	8	/	3	5	9	10	4	6
I_5:	5	10	3	4	6	9	/	2	0	8	7	1	11
Intervals:	7	9	11	9	5	11		1	5	1	3	3	7

and 3,

P₅:	5	0	7	6	4	1	/	8	10	2	3	9	11
I₁₀:	10	3	8	9	11	2	/	7	5	1	0	6	4
Intervals:	7	9	11	9	5	11		1	5	1	3	3	7

Where in the examples cited from Webern and Berg the same sum was maintained between the T-nos. of associated complementary row forms, Schoenberg maintains the same difference (7 in the present instance), since no other relation between complementary forms of the given row produces P and I hexachords of mutually exclusive content. The series of interval numbers produced by the paired row forms will remain unchanged, whereas the preservation of a constant sum for different pairs of T-nos. will result in a new permutation of the series of interval numbers for every change in T-nos. other than the tritone substitution.

The first movement of Schoenberg's Serenade, Opus 23, is an example of a pre-dodecaphonic "atonal" composition that is based on strict inversional complementation.[9] The complementary pitch-class relations upon which the periodic formal design of the exposition depends are represented throughout by a single sum, 4. In this respect the movement foreshadows an aspect of Webern's twelve-tone practice, rather than Schoenberg's.

9. *Ibid.*, pp. 31f.

3. Symmetrical Chords and Progressions

Symmetrical progressions (the simultaneous unfolding of inversionally related pitches) and symmetrical chords (pitch-class collections that may be analyzed into inversionally complementary sub-collections) have been most systematically exploited in some of the works of Béla Bartók, above all the Fourth Quartet.[10]

The primary basic cells of this work, at their principal pitch level, are, in pitch-class number notation,[11]

$$
\begin{array}{lcccc}
x_0: & 0 & 1 & 2 & 3 \\
y_{10}: & 10 & 0 & 2 & 4 \\
z_{8/2}: & 8 & 1 & 2 & 7
\end{array}
$$

Any tetrachord may be bisected into its component dyads in three different ways. Where a tetrachord is symmetrical the three pairs of dyads may be represented by equations that present invariant intervals (i.e., differences) or invariant sums. Cell x_0 may be partitioned into two semitones $(3-2=1-0)$, two whole steps $(3-1=2-0)$, and two symmetrically related dyads, non-equivalent as intervals but equivalent as sums $(3+0=2+1=3)$. Another disposition of two whole steps is found in cell y_0 $(4-2=0-10)$, which may be alternatively analyzed into two "major 3rds" $(4-0=2-10)$ or two symmetrically related non-equivalent intervals $(4+10=2+0=2)$.

A principal thematic idea of the piece is the progression of x_0 into y_{10}. Since the two cells do not have a common axis of symmetry (and cannot have a common axis, regardless of their respective transpositions, the sum of complementation being odd for any transposition of cell x and even for any transposition of cell y), the progression of x into y cannot be symmetrical. However, a nonsymmetrical progression may be symmetrically reflected in a complementary progression, and this is precisely what occurs in the Fourth Quartet. Cell x_0 is replaced by x_9 (the significance of the "minor 3rd" transposition is explained below), and cell y_{10} is replaced by y_8 (a transposition that intersects with three of the four elements of y_{10}). The sum of complementation of the two progressions

---

10. The functions of strict inversional complementation and interval cycles in the Fourth Quartet are discussed in depth in Antokoletz, *op. cit.,* n. 5, above.

11. Since there is no assumption of temporal ordering, we have taken the pitch-class number of the lowest note of a referential form of each cell as its T-no. Two T-nos. are assigned to cell z because its pitch-class content is invariant under tritone transposition.

together is 0, representing an axis of symmetry that is equivalent to the "tone center" of the piece, c, and the only pitch class that is shared by all four tetrachords of the two progressions:[12]

$$x_0|y_{10}: \quad 0 \quad 1 \quad 2 \quad 3 \quad | \quad 10 \quad 0 \quad 2 \quad 4$$

$$x_9|y_8: \quad 0 \quad 11 \quad 10 \quad 9 \quad | \quad 2 \quad 0 \quad 10 \quad 8$$

Cells x and y are characterized by a special property. Both are segments of interval cycles, the one a segment of the interval-1, the other a segment of the interval-2 cycle. Either cell may be transposed in terms of its cyclic interval—cell x by half steps, cell y by whole steps—just as the diatonic scale may be transposed in terms of its cyclic interval, the perfect fifth, to generate a hierarchical ordering among transpositions of a given collection. The first movement of the Fourth Quartet is a sonata-allegro whose formal components are to some extent defined and differentiated by means of such hierarchically ordered transpositions. The first stabilization of cell x at a new pitch level occurs at the conclusion of the exposition (mm. 46–49), and this new pitch level involves a shift of +1, so that the original content of x_0 is minimally altered. The development section commences at mm. 49–50 with a transposition of the original $x_0|y_{10}$ progression by +2, which produces the analogous alteration of the "tonic" version of cell y. At the conclusion of the development section (mm. 85–92) a linear version of cell x at +3—a "remote" relationship in terms of shared pitch-class content—is transposed by successive descending semitones to the "tonic" version of cell x, at which point the recapitulation begins.

Cell z is an instance of a special type of tetrachord whose unique structural implications derive from the presence of an interval couple of two tritones. Each such tetrachord may be interpreted in terms of either of two axes of symmetry, at $T(n)$ and $T(n\pm3)$. A division of cell z into two semitones is represented by the equation $8-7=2-1$, a division into two "perfect 4ths" by the equation $7-2=1-8$, but in each instance the minus sign may be replaced by the plus sign to give us an invariant sum: $8+7=2+1=3$ and $7+2=1+8=9$. According to the former sum the axis of symmetry of cell $z_{8/2}$ is identical with that of cell x_0, the complementary relations of both deriving from P and I semitonal cycles intersecting at $c\#/d$ and $g/a\flat$. But the transposed cell, $z_{11/5}$, may be interpreted as presenting the same complementary relations:

P/I Dyads of Sum 3

$$x_0: \begin{Bmatrix} 0 & 1 \\ 3 & 2 \end{Bmatrix} \qquad z_{8/2}: \begin{Bmatrix} 1 & 8 \\ 2 & 7 \end{Bmatrix} \qquad z_{11/5}: \begin{Bmatrix} 10 & 11 \\ 5 & 4 \end{Bmatrix}$$

12. Since each of the cells is symmetrical, the inversion of any given instance of a cell is equivalent in content to one or another transposition of the referential forms. The complementary relations between the two progressions are represented in the T-nos. if the second progression is given an I designation: Ix_0/Iy_2.

According to sum 9, $z_{8/2}$ and $z_{11/5}$ both derive their complementary relations from P and I cycles intersecting at *e/f* and *a$\sharp$/b*. They may thus be associated with x_3 and x_9, the $T(n\pm3)$ transpositions of x_0:

P/I Dyads of Sum 9

$$x_3: \begin{cases} 3 & 4 \\ 6 & 5 \end{cases} \quad x_9: \begin{cases} 9 & 10 \\ 0 & 11 \end{cases} \quad z_{8/2}: \begin{cases} 7 & 8 \\ 2 & 1 \end{cases} \quad z_{11/5}: \begin{cases} 4 & 11 \\ 5 & 10 \end{cases}$$

Bartók assigns pivotal functions to cells $z_{8/2}$ and $z_{11/5}$, interpreting each to imply either sum of complementation, 3 or 9. Ultimately it is sum 9 that prevails, with *e/f* as a "dominant" axis of symmetry in opposition to the principal "tone center," *c,* which is mainly, but not exclusively (as we have seen above), asserted by procedures that are not dependent on the concept of strict inversional complementation. The first movement opens with *e/f* and other dyads of sum 9; near the beginning of the development section there are statements of cell $z_{11/5}$ which emphasize the dyad *e/f* as the axis of symmetry, and in the following bars this dyad and those symmetrically related to it predominate; the coda (bars 134ff) begins with an ostinato on *e/f* in the inner voices.

Cell z of Bartók's Fourth Quartet is also the basic cell of Berg's *Lulu* and generates Trope I[13] of the opera (ex. 1). One of the two non-identical forms of this trope comprises cell z at all its even T-nos., the other at all its odd T-nos.:

EXAMPLE 1

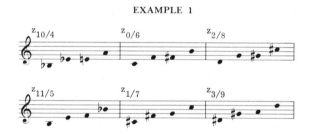

Inversion provides no independent forms, since the generating cell is symmetrical. The properties of cell z that explain its functions in Berg's dodecaphonic opera are the same ones that explain its functions in Bartók's non-dodecaphonic quartet.

In the opening bars of the second movement of Berg's String Quartet, Opus 3, figures based on P/I dyads of sum 8 are embedded among other thematic and harmonic elements (ex. 2). The inversional relations are not always literally expressed, but are sometimes subjected to octave displacements (i.e., complementation is sometimes assumed to determine pitch class, as in the twelve-tone system, rather than pitch) and rhythmic displacements.

13. Perle, *Serial Composition and Atonality,* p. 144.

EXAMPLE 2

Copyright 1925 by Universal Edition, A.G., Vienna.
Renewed 1953 by Helene Berg.
Used by permission.

At bars 28–33 the opening episode culminates in reiterated statements of a motive derived from two sum-8 dyads (ex. 3). The cadential passage which follows repeats the second of these sum-8 dyads through descending octaves and joins to it the remaining notes of the whole-tone segment of bar 5, the last two bars of the episode being entirely limited to the content of that segment. At the conclusion of the exposition (bars 68–71) there is again a return to the same axis of symmetry in a chord made up of two sum-8 dyads (ex. 4). The same collection, however, may be reinterpreted as comprising two sum-2 dyads, and precisely this reinterpretation initiates the development section (ex. 5).

EXAMPLE 3   EXAMPLE 4   EXAMPLE 5

The row of Webern's Symphony consists of two hexachords in the relation $p_0 = r_6$ (ex. 6). The set complex, in this instance, will comprise only twenty-four independent forms, rather than forty-eight, since the P and I sub-complexes will be respectively equivalent to the R and RI sub-complexes.

EXAMPLE 6

But the same row may also be interpreted as comprising three symmetrical tetrachords, and this interpretation plays a very important role. The three tetrachords as comprised in P_9 are ordered versions of Bartók's cells x_6, $z_{11/5}$, x_0. Each tetrachord has the same axis of symmetry, sum 3. The complementary row form that will preserve segmental content is I_6, the combined T-nos. of the paired P and I forms, 9 and 6, giving the required sum of complementation. In example 7 complementary pitch classes of the two row forms are shown in vertical alignment and complementary pitch classes within each row form are joined by ties.

EXAMPLE 7

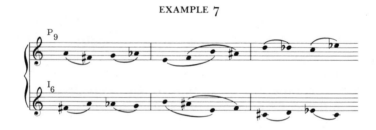

The linear succession of row forms in the first and third double canons of the first movement (bars 1–26 and 43–66) are based on these and corresponding relations. At the same time a second axis of symmetry, 6, determines the relation of vertically associated row forms (cf. p. 6, above), each double canon employing the same eight forms:[14]

$$
\text{Canon I:} \quad
\begin{array}{ll}
P_9 & RI_6 \\
I_9 & R_0
\end{array}
$$

$$
\text{Canon II:} \quad
\begin{array}{ll}
I_5 & R_8 \\
P_1 & RI_{10}
\end{array}
$$

14. *Ibid.*, pp. 118–121.

Wherever a symmetrical tetrachord is complemented at a T-no. that preserves its pitch-class content, it will fall into dyadic segments of invariant content. Variation IV in the second movement of the Symphony is a remarkable example of the compositional exploitation of such invariant dyads.[15]

15. *Ibid.*, ex. 158.

4. Dyadic Sums and Differences

We have seen that the aligned P and I semitonal cycles will produce a collection of symmetrically related dyads representing all the even or all the odd interval numbers, depending on whether the sum of complementary pitch-class numbers is even or odd. One or the other collection, the even or the odd, of symmetrically related intervals is produced wherever there is inversional symmetry, and each such collection will occur in one of its six "keys," signified by one of six even or one of six odd sums. In the following array (Table 1) parallel semitonal cycles are horizontally aligned to produce the twelve transpositions of each interval and opposite semitonal cycles are vertically aligned to produce the six collections of symmetrically related even intervals and the six collections of symmetrically related odd intervals. (The continuation of each row is found by taking the same row again, the continuation of each column by taking the tritone transposition of the same column, i.e., the other column of the same sum.)

The three interval couples into which symmetrical collections of four pitch classes may be partitioned may be read as a pair of dyads that lie in one row of the table, a pair of dyads that lie in another, non-equivalent, row, and a pair of dyads that lie in a single column. Such tetrachords are systematically employed as the basis of Bartók's Fourth Quartet. The work opens with three dyads from the sum-9 column: (4,5) (3,6) (0,9). Two of these form cell x_3, which may also be read in an interval-1 row as (3,4) (5,6), or an interval-2 row as (3,5) (4,6). The tritone transposition, x_9, occurs at the beginning of bar 3 and will be found in the same column and rows. The interval-2 row will also give us one of the three dyadic interpretations of cell y. Column 9 gives us, in addition to cells x_3 and x_9, cell z at both of its primary pitch levels ($z_{8/2}$ and $z_{11/5}$) in the dyadic pairs (4,5) (11,10) and (2,7) (1,8). These may alternatively be read in column 3, as (11,4) (10,5) and (1,2) (8,7). The same column gives us cell x at its primary pitch level in the dyadic pair (0,3) (1,2). The Fourth Quartet derives its tone material and structure largely through such reinterpretations of symmetrical tetrachordal collections.

TABLE 1
Even Sums and Intervals

Sum												
Int.	0=12	2=14	4=16	6=18	8=20	10=22	12=0	14=2	16=4	18=6	20=8	22=10
0/12	0,0	1,1	2,2	3,3	4,4	5,5	6,6	7,7	8,8	9,9	10,10	11,11
2/10	1,11	2,0	3,1	4,2	5,3	6,4	7,5	8,6	9,7	10,8	11,9	0,10
4/8	2,10	3,11	4,0	5,1	6,2	7,3	8,4	9,5	10,6	11,7	0,8	1,9
6/6	3,9	4,10	5,11	6,0	7,1	8,2	9,3	10,4	11,5	0,6	1,7	2,8
8/4	4,8	5,9	6,10	7,11	8,0	9,1	10,2	11,3	0,4	1,5	2,6	3,7
10/2	5,7	6,8	7,9	8,10	9,11	10,0	11,1	0,2	1,3	2,4	3,5	4,6
12/0	6,6	7,7	8,8	9,9	10,10	11,11	0,0	1,1	2,2	3,3	4,4	5,5

Odd Sums and Intervals

Sum												
Int.	1=13	3=15	5=17	7=19	9=21	11=23	13=1	15=3	17=5	19=7	21=9	23=11
1/11	1,0	2,1	3,2	4,3	5,4	6,5	7,6	8,7	9,8	10,9	11,10	0,11
3/9	2,11	3,0	4,1	5,2	6,3	7,4	8,5	9,6	10,7	11,8	0,9	1,10
5/7	3,10	4,11	5,0	6,1	7,2	8,3	9,4	10,5	11,6	0,7	1,8	2,9
7/5	4,9	5,10	6,11	7,0	8,1	9,2	10,3	11,4	0,5	1,6	2,7	3,8
9/3	5,8	6,9	7,10	8,11	9,0	10,1	11,2	0,3	1,4	2,5	3,6	4,7
11/1	6,7	7,8	8,9	9,10	10,11	11,0	0,1	1,2	2,3	3,4	4,5	5,6

5. The Cyclic Set of Interval 7

Adjacencies in the row of the first movement of Berg's *Lyric Suite* generate a complete collection of symmetrically related dyads (of sum 9 for the principal row form):

5　4　　0　9　　7　2　　8　1　　3　6　　10　11

These are compositionally projected in the initial thematic statement of the row and its cyclical permutation (ex. 8).

EXAMPLE 8

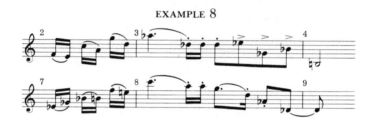

Here we have an exceptional set which is *itself* generated by an alignment of inversionally related cycles. The alternate elements of each hexachord unfold inversionally related segments of interval-7 cycles, aligned as follows for the principal row form. (**Where the aspect of the cycle is not otherwise indicated, P and I cycles will henceforth be differentiated in number notation by the use of italics to represent the former, assuming the reading is from left to right. A retrograde reading, from right to left, converts P into I and I into P.**)

Dyads of Sum 9

5	*0*	*7*	2	9	4	11	6	1	8	3	10	(5
4	9	2	7	0	5	10	3	8	1	6	11	(4

Where a given row form is immediately repeated—an occasional occurrence in the *Lyric Suite* but a regular one in Berg's other work based on the same series, his first twelve-tone composition, *Schliesse mir die Augen beide*—a "secondary set"[16] results from the reversed coupling of hexachords. In that case the paired interval-7 cycles unfold without interrup-

16. *Ibid.*, p. 100.

tion. A continuation of the cycles produces the retrograde form (equivalent to the tritone transposition) and pitch-class repetition at the point where the cycles intersect (ex. 9).

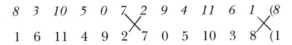

EXAMPLE 9

Berg's row, in the form shown above, displays a special property, uniquely possessed by **sets whose alternate elements unfold complementary cycles of a single interval. We will call these "cyclic sets."** The two pitch classes that are immediate neighbors of any element of the set shown in example 9 always form the same interval, a "perfect 5th" (interval ±7). (In a P cycle each pitch-class number is subtracted from the number that follows it, in an I cycle it is subtracted from the number that precedes it. Thus when the P and I designations are interchanged the above series of pitch-class numbers are defined as interval-5 rather than as interval-7 cycles.)

In example 10 the set is subdivided into its overlapping three-note segments. The "axis note" of each segment (shown in the lower staff) has as its "neighbor notes" the two pitch classes vertically aligned above it in the example. The respective transpositional level of each pair of neighbor notes is inversionally complementary to the respective transpositional level of its axis note.

EXAMPLE 10

6. Cognate Sets

Any given alignment of paired P and I cycles may be read as either a P or an I set form, depending on the order respectively assigned to complementary pitch classes. Paired interval-7 cycles of sum 0, for example, will generate either of the two set forms shown in example 11.

$$0 \quad 7 \quad 2 \quad 9 \quad 4 \quad 11 \quad 6 \quad 1 \quad 8 \quad 3 \quad 10 \quad 5 \quad (0$$

$$0 \quad 5 \quad 10 \quad 3 \quad 8 \quad 1 \quad 6 \quad 11 \quad 4 \quad 9 \quad 2 \quad 7 \quad (0$$

EXAMPLE 11

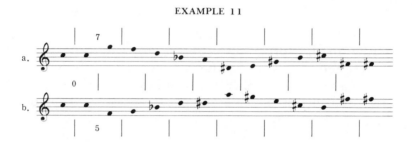

Inversionally related set forms that share a single series of dyads, as in example 11, will be termed "cognate" sets. Each of these may also be interpreted in terms of another alignment of the interval-7 cycles. Example 11,a may be derived from an alignment that generates dyads of sum 7 and example 11,b may be derived from an alignment that generates dyads of sum 5:

Dyads of Sum 7

$$0 \quad 7 \quad 2 \quad 9 \quad 4 \quad 11 \quad 6 \quad 1 \quad 8 \quad 3 \quad 10 \quad 5 \quad (0$$

$$7 \quad 0 \quad 5 \quad 10 \quad 3 \quad 8 \quad 1 \quad 6 \quad 11 \quad 4 \quad 9 \quad 2 \quad (7$$

Dyads of Sum 5

$$5 \quad 0 \quad 7 \quad 2 \quad 9 \quad 4 \quad 11 \quad 6 \quad 1 \quad 8 \quad 3 \quad 10 \quad (5$$

$$0 \quad 5 \quad 10 \quad 3 \quad 8 \quad 1 \quad 6 \quad 11 \quad 4 \quad 9 \quad 2 \quad 7 \quad (0$$

Thus example 11,a has two cognates, one sharing dyads of sum 0 and the other sharing dyads of sum 7 (i.e., 0 plus the cyclic interval); and example 11,b likewise has two cognates, one sharing dyads of sum 0 and the other sharing dyads of sum 5 (i.e., 0 minus the cyclic interval). Each set form of example 11 is shown with its two cognate set forms in example 12.

EXAMPLE 12

Any cyclic set of the set complex may be uniquely identified by its two adjacency sums, which will be used instead of T-nos. to represent the transpositional levels of cyclic set forms. Where the left elements of even dyads and the right elements of odd dyads are members of a P cycle, the set is assumed to be in its prime aspect; where these are members of an I cycle, the set is assumed to be in its inverted aspect. Lower-case letters will be used for the names of cyclic sets. Upper-case letters will henceforth be reserved to identify the aspect of an interval cycle, and an integer following the P or I designation will represent the interval number of the cycle. Example 11,a is thus a p_0p_7 set form, and example 11,b is its cognate, i_5i_0, and both forms are members of the set complex generated by the various alignments of P-7 and I-7 interval cycles. (The difference between the two dyadic sums of a set form is equal to the cyclic interval. Subtract the even sum from the odd for p and vice versa for i. Thus p_0p_7 and i_5i_0 are both interval-7 cyclic set forms. But if the same set forms were respectively named i_7i_0 and p_0p_5, this would indicate that the set was generated by interlocking complementary cycles of interval 5, rather than interval 7. The order in which the sums are named is immaterial: p_0p_7 is the same as p_7p_0, i_5i_0 the same as i_0i_5. To find the alternate sum of a set form, add the cyclic interval number to a given even p sum, subtract it from a given even i sum, and vice versa where the respective sums are odd.)

Example 12 illustrates the alternative cognates of p_0p_7 (ex. 12,a) and i_5i_0 (ex. 12,b), respectively i_7i_2 and $p_{10}p_5$. Since the interval-7 cyclic set in its retrograde aspect is not an independent form, but merely a continuation of the given alignment of the complementary cycles, and since retrograde-related are at the same time tritone-related set forms, the set complex contains only twelve members, six independent primes and six independent inversions, rather than the twenty-four generated by non-cyclic symmetrical sets. In the following series of set forms each member of the complex is preceded and followed by a cognate set form:

P_0P_7 i_7i_2 P_2P_9 i_9i_4 P_4P_{11} $i_{11}i_6$ P_6P_1 i_1i_8 P_8P_3 i_3i_{10} $P_{10}P_5$ i_5i_0 P_0P_7

Elsewhere we have cited examples from Schoenberg and Webern in which the six discrete dyads of a given set form recur in a new order in an inversionally related set form.[17] Cognate set forms in the first movement of the *Lyric Suite* preserve the respective order of invariant dyads. Corresponding passages of the exposition and recapitulation are respectively based on P_5 and its cognate, I_{11}, but the latter is shifted in relation to the former in order to articulate the dyads that I_{11} shares with P_5 (cf. exx. 8 and 13).

EXAMPLE 13

17. *Ibid.*, pp. 117 and 120. See also Perle, "Webern's Twelve-Tone Sketches," *The Musical Quarterly*, LVII (1971), pp. 8f.

7. Verticalization in Twelve-Tone Music[18]

The basic principle of twelve-tone harmony—that adjacent elements of the row may be stated simultaneously, as well as successively, is problematical in a number of respects: (1) The relevance of a verticalized set segment to a given set is ambiguous, the measure of this ambiguity depending on the number of notes in the segment. A succession of six dyads of mutually exclusive pitch-class content, for example, may, in itself, represent any one of 64 different permutations of the twelve notes, while a simultaneity comprising all twelve notes may represent any one of 479,001,600. (2) The possible verticalizations that may be derived from the general set are unsystematic and, from a harmonic point of view, largely fortuitous, and therefore do not lend themselves to any coherent, overall control of the harmonic material. (3) For this reason, the verticalization of set segments, though it is the only general principle of chord structure that has been deduced from the premise of an ordered succession of the twelve notes, cannot be and, in fact, has not been the only criterion of vertical association. Nor do verticalized set segments bear any explicit relation to simultaneities that are otherwise derived, as the triad does to nontriadic elements in tonal music.

I am not aware that Schoenberg, Berg, and Webern ever had anything to say about these problems, but it is obvious enough that, as composers, they were aware of them. Consider Schoenberg's Opus 33a: the three chords which unfold the initial statement of the set may represent any of 13,824 (=4!×4!×4!) different rows. As the work progresses the actual linear ordering on which it is based is unfolded. The original distribution of the twelve notes into a series of tetrads, however, has far more relevance to the composition as a whole than does the serial arrangement of the notes. The general definition of the Schoenbergian set as an ordered succession of the twelve notes of the semitonal scale is obviously inadequate here, for within each tetrad the order is not specified. Simultaneity cannot represent succession, except under arbitrary and excessively restrictive conditions, and for this reason every twelve-tone composition requires a modification of the general definition of the Schoenbergian set. Obviously, this requirement in no way questions the

---

18. This section is taken from *Serial Composition and Atonality*, 2nd ed. (1968), pp. 104–106.

validity of any given twelve-tone work, but it does question the extent to which Schoenberg's method is successful in meeting "the desire for a conscious control of the new means and forms"[19] that led him to formulate this method in the first place.

19. Schoenberg, *op. cit.*, p. 218.

8. Cyclic Chords and Axis-Note Dyads

In one of Schoenberg's last essays he presents the following arguments in support of the attribution of harmonic significance to the general twelve-tone set: "Every tone appears always in the neighbourhood of two other tones in an unchanging combination which produces an intimate relationship most similar to the relationship of a third and a fifth to its root. ... If dissonances other than the catalogued ones are admitted at all in music, it seems that the way of referring them all to the basic set is the most logical and controllable procedure toward this end."[20] But only a very special type of set will generate consistent and coherent adjacency relations and thus function as a "logical and controllable" referential structure for twelve-tone harmony. The principle of verticalization provides no basis for a total and systematic control of the harmonic dimension when it is applied to the general Schoenbergian set, but it will do exactly this when applied to any type of cyclic set.

Let us assume, for example, that inversionally related forms of the interval-7 cycle set are paired. In example 10 an i_9i_4 set form (ex. 9) is partitioned into its overlapping three-note segments. We will pair i_9i_4 and p_0p_7 (ex. 11,a). The equivalent segmentation of the latter is shown in example 14.

EXAMPLE 14

If we align these inversionally related set forms so that their I cycles coincide at the unison, and interpret these unisons as axis notes, the combined neighbor notes will produce the twelve transpositions of a symmetrical tetrachord (ex. 15) whose "primary interval couple" is 7,7 (the cyclic intervals) and "secondary interval couple" is 3,3 (or 9,9). (The name of the secondary interval couple depends on how we choose to read the difference between vertically aligned elements of the two set-forms.

20. *Ibid.*, pp. 246f.

EXAMPLE 15

p₀p₇: *0 0 7 5   2 10 9 3 4 8 11*   1 6 6   *1* 11 8 4 3 9 10 2 5 7 (0

i₉i₄: *9 0 4 5 11* 10 6 3 1 8   8 1 3 6 10 11 5 4 0 9   7 2 2 7 (9

If we realign the two set forms (or reverse their direction) so that the P cycles rather than the I cycles coincide at the unison, the same series of chords occurs (ex. 16), the axis notes now unfolding the combined P cycles and the neighbor-note dyads the combined I cycles.

EXAMPLE 16

p₀p₇: *7 0   0 7 5 2 10 9 3 4 8 11*   1 6 6 *1* 11 8 4 3 9 10   2 5 (7

i₉i₄: *4 0 9 7 2 2   7 9 0 4 5 11* 10 6 3 1   8 8 1 3 6 10 11 5 (4

In example 17 interval 11 replaces the unison as axis-note dyad and interval couple 2,2 replaces 3,3 as the secondary interval couple of **the "cyclic chord" (the chord formed by the neighbor notes). (We will assume that differences are measured in one direction for "axis-note dyads" and in the opposite direction for "neighbor-note dyads.")**

EXAMPLE 17

In example 18 the axis-note interval is 1 and the secondary interval couple of the cyclic chord is 4,4.

EXAMPLE 18

p₀p₇: 7 *0*   0 7 5 2 10   *9*   3 4 8 *11*   1 6 6 *1*   11 8 4 3 *9 10*   2 5 (7

i₉i₄: 3 *1* 8 8 1 *3*   6 *10* 11 5 4   *0* 9 7 2 2   7 9 0 4 5 *11* 10 6 (3

The same series of symmetrical tetrachords is formed in example 19 by axis-note interval 5 and secondary interval couple 8,8 (or, if we assume a complementary reading of interval numbers, axis-note interval 7 and secondary interval couple 4,4).

EXAMPLE 19

p₀p₇: 3 4 8 *11* 1   6   6 *1* 11 8 4 *3* 9 *10* 2   5   7 *0* 0 7 5 2 10 *9* (3

i₉i₄: 7 9 0   4 5 *11* 10 6   3 *1* 8 8 1   *3* 6 *10* 11 5 4 0 9 7   2 2 (7

We will call the paired set forms, in all of its alignments, an "array," and the six-note collections produced by the combined three-note segments of paired set forms "axis-dyad chords." Since axis notes and neighbor notes are derived from opposite cycles, their respective transpositions are inversionally complementary, so that tritone-related axis-note dyads will be associated with inversionally tritone-related cyclic chords. But the inversional complement of a tritone is the tritone. Thus in each of the above examples, 15–19, the first six axis-dyad chords are repeated at the tritone transposition in the six remaining axis-dyad chords.

Not only do paired members of the interval-7 cyclic set complex produce every cyclic chord of primary interval couple 7,7 at every pitch level, but each of these chords is also associated, somewhere in the complex, with axis-note dyads of every interval number, at every pitch level. Thus any six-note collection that contains two interval-7's may be interpreted as a combination of an axis-note dyad and its neighbor notes within the complex of axis-dyad chords generated by the interval-7 cyclic set complex. Let us take the following pitch-class collection:

$$5 \quad 8 \quad 11 \quad 0 \quad 3 \quad 5$$

The two cyclic intervals (the "interval system") are given by 8,3 and 5,0. The remaining elements, 5 and 11, must serve as axis notes. The paired segments will be either 3 *5* 8 and 0 *11* 5, or 3 *11* 8 and 0 *5* 5. Extrapolating the complete set form from each segment by completing the respective P and I interval-7 cycles, we find that the required six-note collection will occur within the series of axis-dyad chords produced by a specific alignment of either of two pairs of set forms:

p_4p_{11}: *2* 2 9   7   *4* | 0 *11* 5 | *6* 10 *1* 3 *8*   8 *3* 1 *10* 6   *5* 11 *0* 4 7 9 (*2*

i_1i_8:   *8* 5 3 10 *10* | 3   5 8 | *0*   1 7 6 2 11 9 4   4 9 *11*   2 6 7 *1* 0 (*8*

$p_{10}p_5$: *8* 2 *3*   7 *10* | 0   5 5 | *0* 10 7 3 2   8 9 1   4 6 *11* 11 6 4 *1* 9 (*8*

i_7i_2:   *2* 5 9 10   *4* | 3 *11* 8 | *6*   1 *1* 6 8 11 *3* 4 *10* 9   *5*   2 0 7 7 0 (*2*

9. Difference Tables

If we take a given difference as the interval number of the axis-note dyad, the differences adjacent to it will produce the secondary interval couple of the cyclic chord. A change in the interval number of the axis-note dyad will always coincide with a complementary change in the secondary interval couple of the cyclic chord. In examples 15–16 the axis interval is 0 and each adjacent secondary interval is 3, in example 17 the respective interval numbers are 11 and 2, in example 18 they are 1 and 4, in example 19 they are 5 and 8. Substituting the complementary interval numbers, we can read the same interval adjacencies as 0 and 9, 1 and 10, 11 and 8, and 7 and 4. **The difference between the axis interval number and either secondary interval number adjacent to it in the paired set forms is in each instance 3, or 9, where the vertically aligned dyadic sums which give the paired set forms their respective names show differences of 3,3, or 9,9, as do p_0p_7/i_9i_4. This pair of integers represents what we will call a "mode." We will assume that the "i" dyadic sums are subtracted from the "p" dyadic sums and say that the given "array," p_0p_7/i_9i_4, is in "Mode 3,3"** of "interval system 7,7." The same mode is represented in other "keys" by $p_{10}p_5/i_7i_2$, p_8p_3/i_5i_0, p_6p_1/i_3i_{10}, p_4p_{11}/i_1i_8, and $p_2p_9/i_{11}i_6$. These will, respectively, reproduce examples 15–19 at $T(5)$ and $T(5)$ plus the tritone, or $T(11)$, $T(4)$ and $T(10)$, $T(3)$ and $T(9)$, $T(2)$ and $T(8)$, and $T(1)$ and $T(7)$.

All the alignments of p_0p_7 and i_9i_4 that were illustrated above are included in Table 2, which is formed by moving each successive statement of one of the alternating set forms two places to the left and each successive statement of the other two places to the right, so that cycles of identical aspect continue to be vertically aligned. The alternating vertical intervals shown in parentheses are derived, in the given array, by subtracting each element of the P cycle of p_0p_7 from the vertically aligned element of the P cycle of i_9i_4, and each element of the I cycle of i_9i_4 from the vertically aligned element of the I cycle of p_0p_7.

TABLE 2

p_0p_7: 0   0 7   5   2 10   9 3   4   8 *11*   1   6   6   *1* 11   8 4   3   9 *10*   2   5   7 *(0*
(7/10)

i_9i_4: 7   2 2   7   *9*   0   4 5 *11* 10   6   3   *1*   8   8   1   *3* 6 *10* 11   5   4   0   9 *(7*
(0/3)

p_0p_7: 7   5 2 10   *9*   3   4 8 *11*   1   6   6   *1* 11   8   4   *3* 9 *10*   2   5   7   0   0 *(7*
(5/8)

i_9i_4: *0*   9 7   2   2   7   *9* 0   4   5 *11* 10   6   3   *1*   8   8 1   *3*   6 *10* 11   5   4 *(0*
(10/1)

p_0p_7: *2* 10 9   3   4   8 *11* 1   6   6   *1* 11   8   4   *3*   9 *10* 2   5   7   0   0   7   5 *(2*
(3/6)

i_9i_4: *5*   4 *0*   9   7   2   2 7   *9*   0   4   5 *11* 10   6   3   *1* 8   8   1   *3*   6 *10* 11 *(5*
(8/11)

p_0p_7: *9*   3 4   8 *11*   1   *6* 6   *1* 11   *8*   4   *3*   9 *10*   2   *5* 7   *0*   0   7   5   2 10 *(9*

The substitution of i_3i_{10} for i_9i_4 converts Table 2 into a representation of Mode 9,9 (Table 3).

TABLE 3

p_0p_7: *0*   0 7   5   2 10   9 3   4   8 *11*   1   6   6   *1* 11   8   4   *3*   9 *10* 2 5   7 *(0*
(4/1)

i_3i_{10}: *4* 11 *11*   4   6   9   *1* 2   8   7   *3*   0 *10*   5   5 10   *0*   3   7   8   2 1 9   6 *(4*
(9/6)

p_0p_7: 7   5 2 10   *9*   3   4 8 *11*   1   *6*   6   *1* 11   8   4   *3*   9 *10*   2   5 7 0   0 *(7*
(2/11)

i_3i_{10}: *9*   6 4 11 *11*   4   6 9   *1*   2   8   7   *3*   0 *10*   5   5 10   *0*   3   7 8 2   1 *(9*
(7/4)

p_0p_7: *2* 10 9   3   4   8 *11* 1   6   6   *1* 11   8   4   *3*   9 *10*   2   5   7   *0* 0 7   5 *(2*
(0/9)

i_3i_{10}: *2*   1 9   6   4 11 *11* 4   6   9   *1*   2   8   7   *3*   0 *10*   5   5 10   *0* 3 7   8 *(2*
(5/2)

p_0p_7: *9*   3 4   8 *11*   1   *6* 6   *1* 11   8   4   *3*   9 *10*   2   5   7   *0*   0   7 5 2 10 *(9*

10. Composing with 12-Tone Modes

The short movement for piano reprinted in its entirety in example 20 is derived from the p_0p_7/i_3i_{10} array. The first bar, letter A, is taken from the intervals 0/9 alignment and combines the three-note segments, 11 *8* 4 / 2 *8* 7. The same axis-dyad chord gives us G and P. At A pitch-class 8 occurs twice, as in the array, but at G and again at P a single statement of 8 represents the common element of the combined segments. At P pitch-class 4 is omitted, but it is contained in the preceding chord and serves as a common boundary element of adjoining three-note segments of p_0p_7: *9* 3 4 8 *11*. In general, where a component of an axis-dyad chord is omitted it may be accounted for in this way, as at B, where pitch-class 7 is missing from axis-dyad chord 4 *3* 9 / (7) *3* 0.

Since the array is produced by pairing inversionally complementary set forms, any pitch-class collection found in the array will be matched by an inversionally complementary collection—or, more precisely, by two such collections separated by the tritone. The sum of complementary sums—p_0 and i_{10}, p_7 and i_3—is 10; the sum of complementary pitches, 5 or 11, is found by dividing this sum, or this sum plus 12, by 2:

p_0p_7:	*0*	0	7	5	2	10	*9*	3	*4*	8	*11*	1	*6*	6
$i_{10}i_3$:	5	*5*	10	*0*	3	7	8	2	1	9	6	4	11	*11*
p_0p_7:	*0*	0	7	5	2	10	9	3	4	8	*11*	1	6	6
$i_{10}i_3$:	11	*11*	4	6	9	*1*	2	*8*	7	3	0	*10*	5	5

The second chord, at B, is related to the first not only in that it is the adjoining axis-dyad chord in the intervals 0/9 alignment, but also in that it is the inversional complement (sum 11) of the first:

A: (p_7p_0) 11 *8* 4 / $(i_{10}i_3)$ 2 *8* 7

B: (i_3i_{10}) *0* 3 7 / (p_0p_7) 9 3 4

It will likewise be an inversional complement (sum 5) of the chord at D, since the latter is a tritone transposition, 5 *2* (10) / 8 *2* 1, of the first chord. (The notes *b*♭ and *d* of letter C seem best explained as an extension of the p_0p_7 segment of B (4 *3* 9 *10* 2).) At E the combined segments, 10 *9* 3 / 1 *9* (6), are a tritone transposition of B and thus

EXAMPLE 20

Perle, Modal Suite, I (1940)

Copyright 1941 by Boletin latino-americano de musica, V.
Used by permission.

inversionally complementary to A and D. Since bars 13–16 recapitulate bars 1–4 in inversion (sum 11), the opening and closing phrases, except for the final cadential chord, are entirely derived from the hexachordal collection in bar 1.

The second phrase introduces a new axis interval, 7, and its mod 12 complement, 5. The combined segments at F are taken from the intervals-5/2 alignment: 4 *3* 9 / 2 *8* 7, a collection which is its own inversional complement (sum 11):

$$(p_7p_0) \quad 4 \quad 3 \quad 9 \; / \quad (i_{10}i_3) \quad 2 \quad 8 \quad 7$$

$$(i_3i_{10}) \quad 7 \quad 8 \quad 2 \; / \quad (p_0p_7) \quad 9 \quad 3 \quad 4$$

The tritone d-a^b overlaps with a restatement of the first chord at G. H and J may be derived from the intervals-7/4 alignment: 11 *8* 4 / 7 *3* 0. This collection, like that which opens the second phrase, is self-invertible, as will be any axis-dyad chord whose axis notes have a sum of 11 or 5. The intervening chord at letter I combines segments of the intervals-5/2 alignment: 2 *5* 7 / 0 *10* 5.

The retransition commences at K with an axis-interval 0 chord, 0 7 5 / 3 7 8, whose pitch-class content largely overlaps with the axis-interval 7 chord at H and J. L returns to an inverted form of the initial collection, the same paired segments which concluded the first phrase: 10 *9* 3 / 1 *9* 6. The same chord brings the retransition to a close as part of a sum-5 inversion (at M and N) of the figure (F and G) which opened the second phrase. M is not only an explicit inversion, but also a T(6) transposition of the content of F: 10 *9* 3 / 8 *2* 1. Thus the two tritones at F, d-a^b and e^b-a, recur at M. The same tritones dominate the opening and closing sections of the movement, each occurring in alternate bars at A through E and O through S.

The final chord combines segments 8 *11* 1 and 11 *11* 4. Pitch-class repetition in the i_3i_{10} segment, due to the coincidence of the axis dyad and an adjacency at this point, limits the collection to four pitch classes, and these are equivalent to a tetrachordal segment of the p_0p_7 set form: 4 8 *11* 1. (In fact, *any* cyclic chord, since it will be formed by the combination of two cyclic intervals, will be equivalent to a tetra-chordal segment of each of two cognate set forms. Thus the above chord will also occur as 8 *4* 1 *11* in i_5i_0.) The two axis notes of the paired segments, 11 and 11, form the principal axis interval, 0, at a transpositional level which makes that interval equivalent to a dyadic segment of the other set form, i_3i_{10}. **Wherever the axis dyad is a segment, as it is here, of one of the two set forms that generate the array (which is to say, wherever its sum is one of the four adjacency sums given in the name of the array), its four neighbor notes will produce a segment of the other set form. Such chords have special functions in the system as a whole and we will refer to them as "tonic chords."** (In example 20 the p_0p_7 segment of the final chord, *e g♯ b,* plays an important structural role as a component of the initial chord of the first phrase and the final chord of the second phrase. The cyclic interval in this instance, *e-b,* is at the same time a dyadic segment of sum 3 of the other set form, i_3i_{10}.)

Example 20 is the earliest composition in the "twelve-tone modal system." As in Schoenberg's system, the tone relations are referable to a specific linear ordering of the semitonal scale. But the cyclic set, unlike the general twelve-tone set, is implied in its entirety by any one of its three-note segments, since each such segment comprises all the criteria that define the set—the alternate sums formed by adjacent pitch classes and the cyclic interval expressed in the difference between these sums. Each such segment may be extended in either direction. Where the axis interval is 0, a given pitch class is represented twice. However, a single compositional representation of that pitch class is often interpreted as a point of intersection between the two set forms, and in example 20 this occurs more or less consistently.

Deviations from the precompositionally assumed ordering of the row in Schoenberg's twelve-tone system are usually "explained" as "licenses." But the procedures that we have described in the preceding analysis of the first movement of the *Modal Suite* are no longer "licenses," since they do not modify the ordering of the set, which is fully represented in each axis-dyad chord of the system. The explicit and literal reiteration of the set as a total linear structure is no more necessary than would be the constant foreground reiteration of the diatonic scale as a means of representing the key of a tonal composition. Of every pitch class in the p_0p_7/i_3i_{10} array, we know that it is cyclically related to two pitch classes at intervals +7 and −7, and serially adjacent to each of four pitch classes with which it forms sums of 0, 7, 3, and 10. The first movement of the *Modal Suite* represents only one of any number of possible compositional interpretations of these relations.[21]

Example 21 is largely based on the same array, and the same alignment of that array, as example 20. The unison axis dyad of the paired segments of the two set forms is indicated in the example by its pitch-class

21. The analysis of this piece as given above is *ex post facto* at a distance of more than thirty years. There was no conscious attempt to exploit certain inherent properties of the system as these are now understood, and to the extent that these are manifest in the composition it is because they are in the nature of the tone material generated by cyclic sets. For example, the "tonic chord" was assigned a special function only because of its pivotal connections with other arrays, as explained below, and the composer was not alert to the significance of the fact that such a chord differs from other neighbor-note collections in that it forms a segment of one of the set forms that is the co-generator of the array in which that chord occurs as one of a complex of symmetrically and transpositionally related axis-dyad chords, if, indeed, he was even aware of the fact itself. And, at the time, the chords were all in principle derived as neighbor-note collections of interval-0 axis notes, though it is now clear that several of them are better explained in other ways.

EXAMPLE 21

Merkin, Five Preludes, I (1976)

Copyright 1977 by Robby Merkin.
Used by permission.

number. Details that cannot be interpreted as paired three-note segments of axis-interval 0 are marked by brackets in the example.

The cyclic chord at the beginning of bar 9 is generated by axis notes of sum 0:

$$p_0p_7: \quad 1 \quad 6 \quad 6$$
$$i_3i_{10}: \quad 4 \quad 6 \quad 9 \quad (1)$$

The axis dyad is thus equivalent to an adjacency in one of the two set forms of the array p_0p_7, and the cyclic chord of this "tonic dyad" will be equivalent in content to a segment of the other set form, i_3i_{10}, as explained above. By assigning the function of axis notes to another pitch class of the same cyclic chord we effect a modulation into another array:

$$i_3i_{10}: \quad 1 \quad 9 \quad 6 \quad (4)$$

$$p_6p_1: \quad 4 \quad 9 \quad 9$$

The new array, p_6p_1/i_3i_{10}, is in Mode 3,3, which is to say that axis-interval 0 will generate cyclic chords of secondary interval couple 3,3. Thus common axis notes produce the same collection of cyclic chords in both arrays, but the axis dyad for any given cyclic chord of the first array is transposed by $T(3)$ in relation to the same chord in the second array, as it was in the tonic chord that served as a pivotal connection between the two arrays. Bars 9–13 are based on the following alignment from the new array:

i_3i_{10}:   4   11   *11*   4   *6*   9   *1*   2   8   7   *3*   0   *10*   5   5   10   *0*   3   7   8   *2*   1   9   6   *(4*   11
    (0/3)

p_6p_1:   4   2   *11*   7   6   0   *1*   5   8   10   *3*   3   *10*   8   5   1   *0*   6   7   11   *2*   4   9   9   *(4*   2

In bars 13–14 the tritone transposition of the earlier pivotal chord serves as a means of effecting a return to the original array:

$$i_3i_{10}: \quad 7 \quad 3 \quad 0 \quad (10)$$

$$p_6p_1: \quad 10 \quad 3 \quad 3$$

$$\overline{}$$

$$p_0p_7: \quad 7 \quad 0 \quad 0$$

$$i_3i_{10}: \quad 10 \quad 0 \quad 3 \quad (7)$$

Conversely, axis notes of sum 10 coincide with dyadic segments of i_3i_{10} and will generate tonic cyclic chords that coincide with segments of p_0p_7. These occur at the conclusion of bar 19,

$$p_0p_7: \quad (4) \quad 8 \quad 11 \quad 1$$

$$i_3i_{10}: \quad\quad\quad 11 \quad 11 \quad 4$$

and, at the tritone transposition, as the penultimate simultaneity of the movement,

$$p_0p_7: \quad (10) \quad 2 \quad 5 \quad 7$$

$$i_3i_{10}: \quad\quad\quad 5 \quad 5 \quad 10$$

Wherever three-note segments are paired to produce cyclic chords of primary interval couple 7,7 (or 5,5) and secondary interval couple 3,3 (or 9,9), we can reinterpret these as derived from cyclic set forms of interval 3 (or 9), aligned to produce alternate vertical dyads of interval 7 (or 5). Thus, to the extent that examples 20 and 21 unfold paired three-note segments sharing a common axis pitch-class, it is possible to assume their derivation from paired interval-3 or interval-9 cyclic set forms. Interval 3 or 9 partitions the twelve pitch classes into three sub-cycles, as follows:

$$0 \quad 3 \quad 6 \quad 9 \quad (0$$
$$1 \quad 4 \quad 7 \quad 10 \quad (1$$
$$2 \quad 5 \quad 8 \quad 11 \quad (2$$

If these are read from left to right as P and from right to left as I, cyclic-interval 3 is implied; the opposite attribution implies the complementary cyclic interval, 9. P and I cycles are aligned as before, to produce dyads of a constant sum. For example:

DYADS OF SUM 0

0   3   6   9 (0   *1   4   7   10* (1
0   9   6   3 (0   11   8   5   2 (11

The alternate sum will be either 3 (=0+3) or 9 (=0−3), depending on the ordering of the P/I dyads of sum 0. The set will fall into two partitions, one of four and the other of eight pitch classes:

p_0p_3:   *0*) 0 *3* 9 6 (6 *9*.. ‖ *1* 11 4 8 7 5 *10* 2 (*1*
i_0i_9:   *0*) *0* 9 *3* 6 (6 *3*.. ‖ 11 *1* 8 4 5 7 2 *10* (11

The following alignments will generate all the chords of axis-interval 0 in example 21. The pivotal tonic chords in bars 9 and 13–14 are indicated by brackets.

p_0p_3:   0 *3* 9 6 6 *9*   3 0 (0 *3*   ‖ *1* 11 4 8 7 5 *10* 2 (*1* 11 ‖
  (0/5)
i_7i_{10}:   7 *3* 4 6 1 *9* 10 0 (7 *3*   ‖ *1*   6 4 3 7 0 *10* 9 (*1*   6 ‖

11 1 2 10 *5* 7 *8*   4 (*11* 1

11 8 2   5 *5* 2 *8* 11 (*11* 8

$p_{10}p_1$:   5   5 *8* 2 *11* 11 2 8 (5   5   ‖ *6* 4 9 1 *0* 10 *3* 7 (*6* 4 ‖
  (0/7)
i_3i_6:   5 10 *8* 7 *11*   4 2 1 (5 10   ‖ *6* 9 9 6 *0*   3 *3* 0 (*6* 9 ‖

4 6 7 3 *10* 0 *1* 9 4   6

4 11 7 8 *10* 5 *1* 2 4 11

At A there is a series of symmetrically related dyads that is most simply explained as an extended segment of the interval-3 set form, i_7i_{10}: *3 4 6 1 9* 10. The associate interval-3 set form, p_0p_3, however, is represented at A only by a single sum-3 dyad, 7 8. The *d* on the third beat of bar 6 re-establishes sum 3 as a component of the interval-7 set form, i_3i_{10}, in the segment 7 8 *2*. At B and C there are extended set segments premised on interval-7 rather than interval-3 cycles. The bracketed collection at B may be explained as unfolding the following segments:

$$i_3i_{10}: \quad 9 \quad 1 \quad 2 \quad 8 \quad 7 \quad 3$$

$$p_6p_1: \qquad\quad 1 \quad 5 \quad 8$$

The axis-dyad chord in bar 16,

$$p_0p_7: \quad (5) \quad 2 \quad 10$$

$$i_3i_{10}: \quad\quad 8 \quad 2 \quad 1$$

overlaps with the bracketed collection at C,

$$p_0p_7: \quad 9 \quad 10 \quad 2 \quad 5 \quad 7$$

$$i_3i_{10}: \qquad\qquad\quad 7 \quad 3 \quad 0$$

The piece consistently exploits the inversional relationships inherent in the array by juxtaposing complementary chords and progressions. These relationships, however, are not explicitly projected compositionally, as they are, for example, in example 20 (cf., in example 20, bars 13–16 with 1–4, and 5–6 with 11–12). The sum of complementary pitch classes for the first array, whether we assume that array to be p_0p_7/i_3i_{10} or p_0p_3/i_7i_{10}, is 5 or 11 (cf. p. 31, above). The juxtaposition of complementary axis notes is determined by 5 as the sum of complementary pitch classes in bars 1–4 (10+7, 2+3, 9+8) and bars 7–8 (3+2) and by 11 as the sum of complementary pitch classes at the return of the original array in bars 14–15 (1+10, 4+7). The sums of complementary pitch classes for the second array are 2 or 8. In bars 9–11 the juxtaposition is based on 2 as the sum of complementary pitch classes (2+0, 6+8); axis-notes 10 in bar 11 and axis-notes 4 in bar 13 produce self-invertible chords based on 8 as the sum of complementary pitch classes. The latter are shown in the following diagram:

$(i_{10}i_3)$	0	*10*	5 /	(p_1p_6)	3	*10*	8
(p_6p_1)	*8*	10	*3* /	(i_3i_{10})	5	10	*0*

$(i_{10}i_3)$	6	*4*	11 /	(p_1p_6)	9	*4*	2
(p_6p_1)	*2*	4	*9* /	(i_3i_{10})	*11*	4	6

The same chords may be derived as follows from the interval-3 set:

$$(p_{10}p_1) \quad 0 \quad 10 \quad 3 \; / \; (i_3i_6) \qquad 5 \quad 10 \quad 8$$

$$(i_6i_3) \qquad 8 \quad 10 \quad 5 \; / \; (p_6p_{10}) \quad 3 \quad 10 \quad 0$$

$$(p_{10}p_1) \quad 6 \quad 4 \quad 9 \; / \; (i_3i_6) \qquad 11 \quad 4 \quad 2$$

$$(i_6i_3) \qquad 2 \quad 4 \quad 11 \; / \; (p_1p_{10}) \quad 9 \quad 4 \quad 6$$

The final chord may be derived as follows from the intervals-5/2 alignment of the principal array. The two axis notes form a tonic dyad (a segment of i_3i_{10}), and the four neighbor notes a tonic cyclic chord (a segment of p_0p_7):

$$p_0p_7: \quad (5) \quad 7 \quad 0 \quad 0$$

$$i_3i_{10}: \qquad \quad 0 \quad 10 \quad 5$$

The preceding tonic chords in the same phrase (the second chords in bars 19 and 20) form a symmetrical progression converging upon the final chord (ex. 22).

EXAMPLE 22

Any two axis-dyad chords in an array, regardless of whether or not they unfold successively along the set forms of the array, may be connected in terms of their common properties—the primary interval couple and the adjacency sums. The compositional exploitation of these background relations involves rhythmic and octave displacement, as in diatonic music, as well as direct compositional statements of these relations. An example of the latter occurs in the first two bars of example 20, where the symmetrical relations of successive set segments are compositionally projected (ex. 23).

EXAMPLE 23

In examples 15–19 the symmetrical relations between axis and neighbor notes of each chord and the next are literally represented in precompositional statements of various axis-dyad chord collections. Each collection unfolds along the cyclic interval, but even here, though in principle there is no compositional interpretation of the ordered collections, a first step in the direction of such an interpretation is unavoidably implied in the alternation, for practical reasons, of "perfect fourths" and "fifths" in what would ideally be a series of one *or* the other exclusively. The compositional interpretation of such collections may be viewed as the last in a series of such steps, each of which imposes additional compositional elements on the original paradigmatic models. A second step toward a compositional interpretation of example 16, for instance, would be the imposition of a voice-leading design by applying the traditional "rule" of elementary tonal harmony respecting the treatment of common tones. Example 16 is thus converted into the following "keyboard harmony exercise:"

EXAMPLE 24

Example 25 illustrates a number of such "keyboard harmony exercises" that may be derived from the same collection of chords. The "whole notes" represent axis dyads of interval 0. Chord connections based on axis-dyad progressions of every interval are illustrated. The brackets show how voice-leading considerations impose larger sequential patterns and give some rhythmic meaning to otherwise unarticulated harmonic successions such as were illustrated in examples 15–19.

Other interpretations of the same collection are shown in example 26, which illustrates chord progressions based on shared dyads, each consisting of an interval-0 axis note and one neighbor note. Each interval-0 axis note is paired in turn with each of its neighbors in the example. The note *c,* for instance, is paired with its interval-9 neighbor in example 26,a, with its interval-7 neighbor in example 26,b, with its interval-0 neighbor in example 26,c, and with its interval-4 neighbor in example 26,d. In examples 26,c and 26,d smoother voice leading results if an exception is made of the traditional common-tone "rule."

EXAMPLE 25

EXAMPLE 26

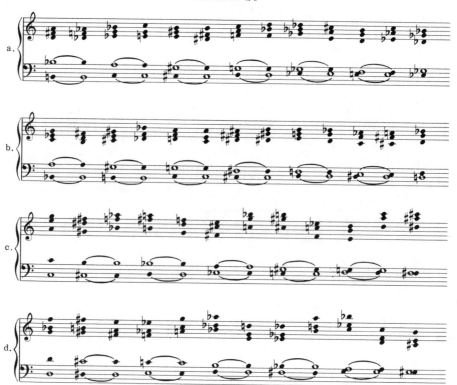

11. The Odd and
Even Modes

The complete collection of modes produced by pairing inversionally related forms of the interval-7 cyclic set is found by combining $p_{2n}p_{2n+7}$ with $i_{2n-1}i_{(2n+7)-1}$ for Mode 1,1; with $i_{2n-3}i_{(2n+7)-3}$ for Mode 3,3; and so on for Modes 5,5; 7,7; 9,9; and 11,11. Each such mode, since it consists of inversionally related set forms, is self-invertible at a given sum of complementation and the same sum ±6 (see p. 31, above). Another collection of modes is formed where set forms of like aspect are combined. The $p_0p_7/p_{10}p_5$ array, for example, will generate the cyclic chords of examples 18–19 in association with axis-intervals 2 and 6. If we assume that the sums of $p_{10}p_5$ are respectively subtracted from those of p_0p_7, the mode, designated by the differences, will be 2,2 (Table 4).

Combining $p_{2n}p_{2n+7}$ with each of its transpositions in turn, we derive the following collection of even-numbered modes:

$$0,0: \quad p_{2n}p_{2n+7}/p_{2n}p_{2n+7}$$

$$2,2: \quad p_{2n}p_{2n+7}/p_{2n-2}p_{(2n+7)-2}$$

$$4,4: \quad p_{2n}p_{2n+7}/p_{2n-4}p_{(2n+7)-4}$$

$$6,6: \quad p_{2n}p_{2n+7}/p_{2n-6}p_{(2n+7)-6}$$

$$8,8: \quad p_{2n}p_{2n+7}/p_{2n-8}p_{(2n+7)-8}$$

$$10,10: \quad p_{2n}p_{2n+7}/p_{2n-10}p_{(2n+7)-10}$$

Modes 8,8 and 10,10 are transpositionally equivalent to 4,4 and 2,2 respectively. Paired set forms of the same aspect will thus generate only four, rather than six, independent modes. The inversionally complementary modes will be found in the modes produced by the inversionally complementary set forms and may be formed by the addition of a constant odd integer to each sum of the original array or any transposition of the latter. The $p_0p_7/p_{10}p_5$ array, for example, is inverted in i_3i_{10}/i_1i_8, i_5i_0/i_3i_{10}, etc. The two inversionally related arrays are complementary forms of Modes 2,2 (or 10,10).

TABLE 4

p₀p₇: *0* 0 7 5 2 10 *9* 3 4 8 *11* 1 *6* 6 *1* 11 *8* 4 *3* 9 *10* 2 5 7 (*0*
(7/5)

p₁₀p₅:*5* 5 *0* 10 7 3 2 8 9 1 *4* 6 *11* 11 6 4 *1* 9 8 2 *3* 7 *10* 0 (5
(2/0)

p₀p₇: *7* 5 2 10 9 3 4 8 *11* 1 *6* 6 *1* 11 *8* 4 *3* 9 *10* 2 5 7 0 0 (7
(9/7)

p₁₀p₅:*0* 0 *5* 5 *0* 10 7 3 2 8 9 1 *4* 6 *11* 11 6 4 *1* 9 8 2 *3* 7 (*10*
(4/2)

p₀p₇: *2* 10 *9* 3 4 8 *11* 1 *6* 6 *1* 11 8 4 *3* 9 *10* 2 5 7 *0* 0 7 5 (*2*
(11/9)

p₁₀p₅:*3* 7 *10* 0 *5* 5 *0* 10 7 3 2 8 9 1 *4* 6 *11* 11 6 4 *1* 9 8 2 (*3*
(6/4)

p₀p₇: *9* 3 *4* 8 *11* 1 *6* 6 *1* 11 *8* 4 *3* 9 *10* 2 5 7 0 0 7 5 2 10 (*9*
(1/11)

p₁₀p₅:*8* 2 *3* 7 *10* 0 *5* 5 *0* 10 7 3 2 8 9 1 *4* 6 *11* 11 6 4 *1* 9 (*8*

12. Sum Tables

The symmetrically related tonic chords illustrated in example 22 were explained above as deriving from two different alignments of p_0p_7/i_3i_{10}:

$$p_0p_7: \quad 8 \quad 11 \quad 1 \quad . \quad . \quad . \quad 2 \quad 5 \quad 7$$
$$(0/9)$$
$$i_3i_{10}: \quad 11 \quad 11 \quad 4 \quad . \quad . \quad . \quad 5 \quad 5 \quad 10$$

$$p_0p_7: \quad 7 \quad 0 \quad 0$$
$$(5/2)$$
$$i_3i_{10}: \quad 0 \quad 10 \quad 5$$

If in each of these chords we assume a reversal of the direction of one of its two segments, so that elements of opposite rather than parallel cycles are vertically aligned, we will find that all three chords can be derived from a single alignment which generates alternating *sums* of 10 and 0,

$$p_0p_7: \quad 9 \; 3 \; 4 \; \boxed{8 \; 11 \; 1} \; 6 \; 6 \; 1 \; 11 \; 8 \; 4 \; 3 \; 9 \; 10 \; \boxed{2 \; 5 \; 7} \; 0 \; 0 \; 7 \; 5 \; 2 \; 10 \; (9 \; 3$$
$$i_{10}i_3: \quad 1 \; 9 \; 6 \; \boxed{4 \; 11 \; 11} \; 4 \; 6 \; 9 \; 1 \; 2 \; 8 \; 7 \; 3 \; 0 \; \boxed{10 \; 5 \; 5 \; 10 \; 0} \; 3 \; 7 \; 8 \; 2 \; (1 \; 9$$

rather than from two different alignments, one generating alternate differences of 0 and 9 and the other alternate differences of 5 and 2. **Where formerly the adjacency sums 0 and 7 were respectively aligned with 3 and 10 to give us a repeated difference, 9,9, that defines the mode, we now find the adjacency sums 0 and 7 respectively aligned with 10 and 3, to give us a repeated sum, 10,10, which defines what we will call the "key" of the given array.**

The complete collection of difference alignments and the complete collection of sum alignments of a given pair of set forms will each generate the same totality of axis-dyad chords—only their distribution will be changed—and unless the type of distribution is specified the term "array" is understood to include both. The difference representation of the p_0p_7/i_3i_{10} array (p. 30, above) may be transformed into the following sum representation (Table 5) by shifting each statement of i_3i_{10} of the former one place to the left. The sum of each pair of newly aligned axis notes and either vertical sum adjacent to it will always be 10, the repeated sum that determines the key.

TABLE 5

p_0p_7:0 0 7 5 2 10 9 3 4 8 *11* 1 *6* 6 *1* 11 *8* 4 *3* 9 *10* 2 *5* 7 *(0*
(11/11)

$i_{10}i_3$:11 *11* 4 *6* 9 *1* 2 *8* 7 *3* 0 *10* 5 5 10 *0* 3 7 8 *2* 1 9 6 *4* (11
(6/4)

p_0p_7:7 5 2 10 *9* 3 4 8 *11* 1 6 6 *1* 11 *8* 4 *3* 9 *10* 2 *5* 7 *0* 0 *(7*
(1/9)

$i_{10}i_3$:6 *4* 11 *11* 4 *6* 9 *1* 2 8 7 3 0 10 5 *5* 10 *0* 3 7 8 2 1 *9* (6
(8/2)

p_0p_7:2 10 *9* 3 4 8 *11* 1 *6* 6 *1* 11 *8* 4 *3* 9 *10* 2 *5* 7 *0* 0 7 5 *(2*
(3/7)

$i_{10}i_3$: 1 *9* 6 *4* 11 *11* 4 *6* 9 *1* 2 8 7 3 0 *10* 5 5 10 *0* 3 7 8 2 (1
(10/0)

p_0p_7:9 3 4 8 *11* 1 6 6 *1* 11 *8* 4 *3* 9 *10* 2 5 7 *0* 0 7 5 2 10 *(9*
(5/5)

$i_{10}i_3$: 8 *2* 1 9 6 *4* 11 *11* 4 *6* 9 *1* 2 8 7 *3* 0 *10* 5 5 10 *0* 3 7 (8

13. Tonic and Resultant Set Forms

Let us take the p_0p_7/i_9i_4 alignment that generates the axis-dyad chords illustrated in example 15 and shift p_0p_7 one degree to the right so that elements of opposite cycles are vertically aligned:

p_0p_7:   7 0 0 7   5   2 10 9 3 4 8 *11* 1 6   6   *1* 11 8 4 3 9 *10* 2 5 (7

i_4i_9:   9 0 4 5 *11* 10   6 3 1 8 8   1 3 6 *10* 11   5 4 0 9 7   2 2 7 (9

Where we previously found alternate differences of 3 and 0 between vertically aligned pitch-class numbers, we now find alternate sums of 4 and 0. Example 27 illustrates the series of chords that is generated if we read successive dyads of sum 0 as axis dyads.

EXAMPLE 27

The collection of symmetrical tetrachords formed by the combined neighbor-note dyads will present, in addition to the primary interval couple (7,7), a characteristic sum couple (4,4), instead of a characteristic secondary interval couple as in example 15. A realignment that produces alternate sums of 5 and 11 will generate cyclic chords of sum-couple 5,5 if we take 11 as the axis-dyad sum (ex. 28).

EXAMPLE 28

p_0p_7: 0 0 7 5 2 10 9 3 4 8 *11* 1 6 6 *1* 11 8 4 *3* 9 *10* 2 5 7 (0

i_4i_9:   5 *11* 10 6 3 *1* 8 8 *1 3* 6 *10* 11 5 4 *0* 9 7 2 2   7 9 0 4 (5

It was pointed out above that every cyclic chord is transpositionally equivalent to a tetrachordal segment of the set. Since each cyclic chord in example 27 has the sum couple 4,4 (as well as the primary interval couple 7,7), it occurs as a segment of one of the two set forms of the given array, i_4i_9. Since the axis dyads of these chords are each of sum 0 they simultaneously occur as segments of the other set form of the array, p_0p_7 (p. 33). Thus every chord in example 27 conforms to our definition of a tonic chord. Example 29 shows how the axis-dyad chords in example 27 unfold the two set forms of the array.

EXAMPLE 29

The key of the p_0p_7/i_9i_4 array is 4,4, since these are the sums of the paired adjacencies, represented by the integers 0 and 4, 7 and 9, in the sum version of the array. Example 30 shows how example 28 may be interpreted not as unfolding dyadic and tetrachordal segments of these set forms but, instead, of two others in the same set complex, whose adjacency sums, 5 and 11, 10 and 6, give us the same key, 4,4. The set forms unfolded in example 30, $p_{10}p_5$ and $i_{11}i_6$, are inversionally complementary to each other at the same sum (2 or 8) as the paired set forms, p_0p_7 and i_9i_4, that generate the array.

EXAMPLE 30

Chords whose axis dyads and neighbor-note collection are equivalent to segments of the set forms that generate the array (we will call these the "tonic" set forms) as in example 27, are hierarchically superior to those that represent other ("resultant") members of the set complex, as in example 28. Whichever resultant set forms are represented in the cyclic chords and axis dyads generated by a specific alignment of the tonic set forms, progression in terms of adjacency relations unfolds the tonic set forms at the same time, and the four adjacency sums of the latter continue to be represented in the relations of each cyclic chord to its axis dyad.

If sum 4 is taken for the axis dyads in the alignment that produced example 27 the two tonic set forms of example 29 are interchanged (ex. 31).

EXAMPLE 31

The following alignment of p_0p_7/i_9i_4 transposes the cyclic chords of example 28 a semitone upward and its axis dyads the same distance in the opposite direction (ex. 32).

EXAMPLE 32

p_0p_7:   *1* 11   *8 4 3* 9 *10* 2 5 7 *0* 0 7 5 2 *10*   9 3 4 8 *11* 1 6 6 (*1*

i_4i_9:   6 *10* 11 *5* 4 *0*   9 7 *2 2* 7 9 0 4 5 *11* 10 6 3 *1*   8 8 1 *3* (6

The new alignment yields the other two tonic sums of the array, 7 and 9, and unfolds the tonic set forms as follows (ex. 33):

EXAMPLE 33

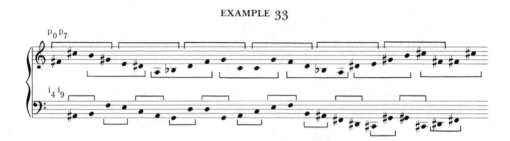

A reinterpretation of the same alignment, assigning sum 7 to the axis dyads, interchanges the two tonic set forms (ex. 34). Examples 29, 31, 33, and 34 comprise all the tonic cyclic chords and all the tonic axis dyads of the p_0p_7/i_9i_4 array.

EXAMPLE 34

14. Sum Tetrachords

We have formed tetrachordal collections by aligning three-note segments of two set forms and omitting the middle column of each pair of segments, so that only the cyclic intervals are represented. In example 35 we illustrate another type of tetrachordal collection. We have taken the same alignment of p_0p_7/i_9i_4 from which we derived example 15 and combined what we have been calling an "axis dyad" with only one pair of its neighbor notes—those to its right in this instance. The individual chords are no longer characterized by the primary interval couple, 7,7, nor by the secondary interval couple that defines the specific alignment of the respective cycles of the paired set forms, 3,3. Instead we find a characteristic sum couple, 7,4, which we will call a "primary" sum couple since it includes one of the alternate adjacency sums of each of the tonic set forms, and an interval couple, 0,3, which characterizes the specific alignment.

EXAMPLE 35

The complete p_0p_7/i_9i_4 difference table (Table 2) rotates the series of sum-7 and the series of sum-4 adjacencies relative to each other so that each dyadic representative of either sum is joined at some point with each dyadic representative of the other, to form all possible tetrachords of sum couple 7,4. **We may regard the array, partitioned into sum 4 and sum 7 adjacencies, as a collection of all possible settings of a slide rule consisting of two sum scales:**

Sum 7: 0,7 5,2 10,9 3,4   8,11 1,6 6,1 11,8 4,3   9,10 2,5 7,0 (0,7

Sum 4: 2,2 7,9 0,4 5,11 10,6 3,1 8,8 1,3 6,10 11,5   4,0 9,7 (2,2

In addition to the primary sums of the array, 7 and 4, there will be a "secondary" sum couple that characterizes the specific setting. The setting of the two sum scales as given above has the secondary sum couple 2,9 (the sums of diagonally opposite pitch classes of each tetrachord), and the characteristic interval couple 10,7. If the slide-rule setting is changed by a shift of the sum-4 scale three degrees to the right,

Sum 7:   0,7 5,2 10,9 3,4 8,11 1,6 6,1   11,8 4,3 9,10 2,5 7,0   (0,7

Sum 4:   11,5 4,0   9,7 2,2 7,9   0,4 5,11 10,6 3,1 8,8   1,3 6,10 (11,5

the secondary sum couple becomes 5,6 and the interval couple becomes 1,10. The sum of the secondary sums will always equal the sum of the primary sums (11); the difference between the interval numbers will always equal the difference between the primary sums (3). **The sum interpretation of the characteristic interval couple (we will call this the "tertiary" sum couple) changes from chord to chord by the addition of a constant depending on the cyclic interval.** In the present instance that constant is 2(−7), 2(+7). In the above slide-rule setting, for example, the successive tertiary sum couples would be 11,0/9,2/ etc.

Similarly, we may segment the two set forms into their respective adjacencies of sums 0 and 9. The difference table comprises all the slide-rule settings of the following sum scales:

Sum 0:   0,0 7,5 2,10 9,3   4,8 11,1 6,6 1,11 8,4   3,9 10,2 5,7 (0,0

Sum 9:   2,7 9,0 4,5   11,10 6,3   1,8 8,1 3,6 10,11 5,4   0,9 7,2 (2,7

The primary sum couple of each tetrachord, whatever the setting, will be 0,9; the illustrated setting produces tetrachords of secondary sum couple 7,2 and interval-couple 2,5.

We may likewise derive a collection of tetrachords by combining vertically aligned adjacencies of the sum representation of the same array (Table 6).

The different settings of the following slide-rule scales will generate tetrachords whose primary sum couple is 0,4:

Sum 0:   0,0 7,5 2,10 9,3   4,8 11,1 6,6 1,11 8,4   3,9 10,2 5,7 (0,0

Sum 4:   2,2 7,9 0,4   5,11 10,6   3,1 8,8 1,3   6,10 11,5   4,0 9,7 (2,2

The given setting is specifically characterized by the secondary sum couple 2,2 (the sums of vertically aligned pitch classes) and the interval couple 2,10 (the differences between diagonally opposite pitch classes of each tetrachord). From the following slide-rule scales we derive all the tetrachords of primary sum couple 7,9:

Sum 7:   0,7 5,2 10,9   3,4   8,11 1,6 6,1 11,8   4,3   9,10 2,5 7,0 (0,7

Sum 9:   2,7 9,0   4,5 11,10 6,3   1,8 8,1   3,6 10,11 5,4   0,9 7,2 (2,7

TABLE 6

p_0p_7:0   0 7 5 2 10 9 3 4 8 *11* 1 6 6 *1* 11 8 4 *3* 9 *10* 2 5 7 (0
(2/2)

i_4i_9: 2   2 7 9 0 4 5 *11* 10 6 3 *1* 8 8 1 *3* 6 *10* 11 *5* 4 *0* 9 7 (2
(9/7)

p_0p_7:7   5 2 10 9 3 4 8 *11* 1 6 6 *1* 11 8 4 *3* 9 *10* 2 5 7 0 0 (7
(4/0)

i_4i_9: 9   7 2 2 7 9 0 4 5 *11* 10 6 3 *1* 8 8 1 *3* 6 *10* 11 *5* 4 0 (9
(11/5)

p_0p_7:2   10 9 3 4 8 *11* 1 6 6 *1* 11 8 4 *3* 9 *10* 2 5 7 0 0 7 5 (2
(6/10)

i_4i_9: 4   *0* 9 7 2 2 7 9 0 4 5 *11* 10 6 3 *1* 8 8 1 *3* 6 *10* 11 5 (4
(1/3)

p_0p_7:9   3 4 8 *11* 1 6 6 *1* 11 8 4 *3* 9 *10* 2 5 7 0 0 7 5 2 10 (9
(8/8)

i_4i_9:11   *5* 4 *0* 9 7 2 2 7 *9* 0 4 5 *11* 10 6 3 *1* 8 8 1 *3* 6 *10* (11

The given setting is specifically characterized by secondary sum couple 2,2 and interval couple 7,5.

Axis-dyad chords are the smallest collections which will completely represent the sums and differences that generate a given array. The series of tetrachords in example 35 unfolds the two set forms of the array in that the omitted cyclic intervals are expressed in the progression from each chord to the next. However, the degree to which any given moment in a composition *must* be representative of the key and the mode of the work is no more predetermined for twelve-tone tonality than it is for diatonic tonality. But wherever it *is* fully representative an axis-dyad chord will be uninterruptedly present in some sort of distribution among the simultaneities and melodic details of which that moment consists.

In itself, a cyclic chord is equally representative of *any* pair of set forms of the given interval system. A sum chord, on the other hand, while it partially identifies the specific set forms, does not identify the interval system of which they are members, since it omits the cyclic intervals. The following settings of slide-rule scales, for example, all produce tetrachords of primary sum couple 7,9, secondary sum couple 8,8, and interval couple 11,1, though the first setting is based on cycles of interval 7, the second on cycles of interval 1, and the third on cycles of interval 2:

Sum 7:	2,5	7,0	0,7	5,2	10,9	3,4	8,11	1,6	6,1	11,8	4,3	9,10	(2,5
Sum 9:	6,3	1,8	8,1	3,6	10,11	5,4	0,9	7,2	2,7	9,0	4,5	11,10	(6,3

Sum 7:	2,5	1,6	0,7	11,8	10,9	9,10	8,11	7,0	6,1	5,2	4,3	3,4	(2,5
Sum 9:	6,3	7,2	8,1	9,0	10,11	11,10	0,9	1,8	2,7	3,6	4,5	5,4	(6,3

Sum 7:	2,5	0,7	10,9	8,11	6,1	4,3	(2,5
Sum 9:	6,3	8,1	10,11	0,9	2,7	4,5	(6,3

15. The Cyclic Set of Interval 1

Example 36 is taken from a piano piece based on the interval-1 cyclic set complex.

EXAMPLE 36

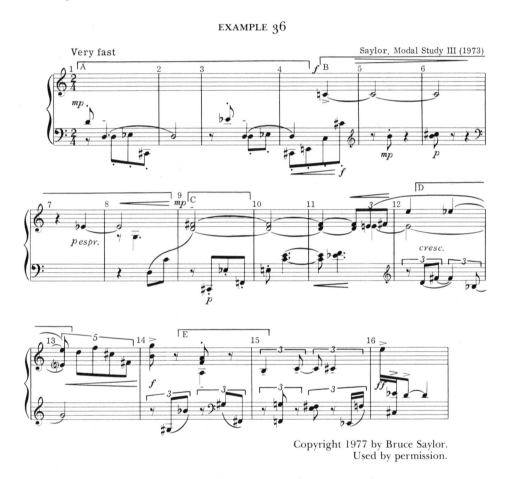

Saylor, Modal Study III (1973)

Copyright 1977 by Bruce Saylor.
Used by permission.

The first four bars would appear to derive from a single set form, p_4p_5. But *any* direct statement of a single set form may be interpreted as a succession of tonic axis-dyad chords in a Mode 0,0 array. The following sum alignment of p_4p_5/p_4p_5 produces alternate tonic axis dyads of sums 5 and 4 and corresponding tonic cyclic chords of primary sum couples 4,4 and 5,5:

p_4p_5: 2 2 3 1 4 . . .

p_5p_4: 2 3 1 4 0 . . .

Taking bars 1–6, a more likely derivation is suggested:

p_4p_5: 2 2 3 1 4 0

i_3i_4: 2 1 3 0 4 11

The addition of bars 7–8 suggests still another array that will serve not only the preceding bars, but that also proves to be highly relevant to the excerpt as a whole (Table 7).

TABLE 7

p_6p_7: 3 3 4 2 5 1 6 0 7 11 8 10 9 9 10 8 11 7 0 6 1 5 2 4 (3
(1/11)

p_4p_5: 2 2 3 1 4 0 5 11 6 10 7 9 8 8 9 7 10 6 11 5 0 4 1 3 (2
(2/0)

p_6p_7: 4 2 5 1 6 0 7 11 8 10 9 9 10 8 11 7 0 6 1 5 2 4 3 3 (4
(3/1)

p_4p_5: 1 3 2 2 3 1 4 0 5 11 6 10 7 9 8 8 9 7 10 6 11 5 0 4 (1
(4/2)

p_6p_7: 5 1 6 0 7 11 8 10 9 9 10 8 11 7 0 6 1 5 2 4 3 3 4 2 (5
(5/3)

p_4p_5: 0 4 1 3 2 2 3 1 4 0 5 11 6 10 7 9 8 8 9 7 10 6 11 5 (0
(6/4)

p_6p_7: 6 0 7 11 8 10 9 9 10 8 11 7 0 6 1 5 2 4 3 3 4 2 5 1 (6
(7/5)

p_4p_5: 11 5 0 4 1 3 2 2 3 1 4 0 5 11 6 10 7 9 8 8 9 7 10 6 (11

Bars 1–9 may be derived from three axis-dyad chords of the p_6p_7/p_4p_5 array:

```
         ┌─── A ───┐      ┌─── B ───┐┌─── C ───┐
$p_6p_7$:  2  4  3      |  11  7  0   6  1  5  (2)
$p_4p_5$:  1  3  2 (2)  |   1  3  2   2  3  1
```

In each of the above interpretations the initial chord is a tonic cyclic chord, equivalent to a segment of p_4p_5 (2 2 3 1), with a tonic axis dyad of sum 5 in the first instance, sum 3 in the second, and sum 7 in the third. The cyclic chord in bar 9 is a segment of p_6p_7 and thus a tonic chord as well. Its tonic axis dyad of sum 4 is reinterpreted,

p_8p_9: 6 3 5

p_6p_7: 2 5 1 (6)

to effect a modulation to a new array (Table 8).

Twelve-Tone Tonality   57

TABLE 8

p₈p₉: *4* 4 5 *3* 6 2 7 1 *8* 0 9 11 *10* 10 *11* 9 *0* 8 *1* 7 2 6 *3* 5 (*4*
 (1/11)

p₆p₇: *3* 3 4 *2* 5 1 6 0 7 11 8 10 9 9 *10* 8 *11* 7 0 6 *1* 5 2 4 (*3*
 (2/0)

p₈p₉: *5* 3 6 *2* 7 1 8 0 9 11 *10* 10 *11* 9 *0* 8 *1* 7 2 6 *3* 5 *4* 4 (*5*
 (3/1)

p₆p₇: *2* 4 3 *3* 4 2 5 1 6 0 7 11 8 10 9 9 *10* 8 *11* 7 0 6 *1* 5 (*2*
 (4/2)

p₈p₉: *6* 2 7 *1* 8 0 9 11 *10* 10 *11* 9 *0* 8 *1* 7 2 6 *3* 5 *4* 4 *5* 3 (*6*
 (5/3)

p₆p₇: *1* 5 2 *4* 3 3 4 2 5 1 6 0 7 11 8 10 9 9 *10* 8 *11* 7 0 6 (*1*
 (6/4)

p₈p₉: *7* 1 8 *0* 9 11 *10* 10 *11* 9 *0* 8 *1* 7 2 6 *3* 5 *4* 4 *5* 3 *6* 2 (*7*
 (7/5)

p₆p₇: *0* 6 *1* 5 2 4 3 3 4 2 5 1 6 0 7 11 8 10 9 9 *10* 8 *11* 7 (*0*

The second array is a T(1)/T(7) transposition of the first. Thus there is a change of key, from 11,11 to 3,3. The mode (2,2), however, remains the same. The *c-e* in bar 10 is a continuation of the reinterpreted set segments of bar 9:

p₈p₉: 6 *3* 5   4

p₆p₇: 2 *5* 1 *6* 0

The suspended *d-f♯* is reinterpreted as a sum-8 dyad and leads in bar 11 to a literal unfolding of a six-note segment of the new set form:

p₈p₉: 2 6 *3* 5 *4* 4

At letter D we have a tonic chord in the new key, but this will not account for the *b♭* in the left hand part:

p₈p₉: 7 2 6 (*3*)

p₆p₇: 3 4 2

The interpolation of the *b♭* between *f♯* and *g* gives a second meaning to these notes, by re-associating them with the displaced set form of the first array:

p₄p₅: 7 *10* 6

There is, in fact, a return to the first array in bar 14, so it is not unreasonable, perhaps, to describe the *b♭* as an anticipation of p₄p₅, especially since the latter, upon its explicit return in bar 14, continues with the adjoining segment, 8 *9* 7. At bar 13 the upper line recapitulates the pitch-class collection in bar 9. The cyclic chord is the same one that served as a pivot to a new array at letter C, associated at this point (because of the half-note *g* in the left-hand part) with still another tonic axis dyad:

$$p_8p_9: \qquad 1 \quad 7 \quad 2$$

$$p_6p_7: \quad (2) \quad 5 \quad 1 \quad 6$$

In the first half of bar 14 a pivotal cyclic chord restores the first array:

$$p_8p_9: \quad 10 \quad 10 \quad 11$$

$$p_6p_7: \quad 7 \quad 11 \quad 8 \quad (10)$$

$$p_6p_7: \quad 10 \quad 8 \quad 11 \quad (7)$$

$$p_4p_5: \quad 7 \quad 9 \quad 8$$

The axis-dyad chord at letter E overlaps with both of its neighbors:

$$p_7p_6: \quad 9 \quad 10 \quad 8$$

$$p_4p_5: \quad 5 \quad 11 \quad 6$$

A series of axis-interval 0 chords begins with the last two notes of bar 14:

$$p_6p_7: \quad 8 \quad 11 \quad 7 \quad 0 \quad 6 \quad 1 \quad 5 \quad | \qquad 3 \quad 3 \quad 4$$

$$p_4p_5: \quad 6 \quad 11 \quad 5 \quad 0 \quad 4 \quad 1 \quad 3 \quad | \quad (4) \quad 1 \quad 3 \quad 2$$

The last bar may also be interpreted as a return to the axis-dyad chord at A:

$$p_6p_7: \quad 2 \quad 4 \quad 3$$

$$p_4p_5: \quad 1 \quad 3 \quad 2 \quad (2)$$

16. Larger Implications of Tonic Set Forms

Bars 1–15 of example 37,a, are derived, like example 36, from several arrays that share a tonic set form. Let us suppose that this set form is combined in turn with each member of the set complex. Table 9 shows the mode and key of each of the resulting arrays. The fourth column shows the tonic cyclic chord that is produced where the axis-dyad interval is 0 and the axis-dyad sum is an adjacency sum of the second set form. The succession of cyclic chords in the column are equivalent in pitch-class content to overlapping segments of the shared set form, p_4p_5. Any other recurring axis-dyad interval that is equivalent to an adjacency of the second set form of each array will similarly produce a series of tonic cyclic chords that unfold the shared set form, as illustrated for axis-interval 5 in the last column.

Examples 27 and 29, 31, 32 and 33, and 34 demonstrated how, within a single array, a series of cyclic chords unfolds the two set forms that generate the array. Where a number of arrays share a tonic set form, as in the above table, the properties of that set form affect the larger formal relations of a composition, as well as its immediate details. No two arrays in the table are in the same key, in the special sense in which we have used this term previously, but there is a high degree of relatedness among all the arrays in the table, since the adjacency sums 4 and 5 are components of every array. In the Toccata p_4p_5 and i_3i_4 are assigned analogous functions. The latter set form is similarly paired with various members of the set complex to form a second collection of arrays. Since they hold adjacency-sum 4 in common, p_4p_5 and i_3i_4 are cognate tonic set forms of the composition as a whole, not merely set forms of individual arrays. The dyads of sum 4 intersect at d and $g\#$. The former is assigned priority as the principal tone center of the work.

We have seen that it is often possible to choose among several plausible readings in tracing a compositional statement to its pitch-class source in an array. Any axis-dyad chord may be derived from either a sum or a difference alignment. The same compositional details may often be analyzed into sum chords in one reading and into axis-dyad chords in another. Where the compositional statement of an axis-dyad chord is incomplete it may often be derived with equal logic from several different alignments of the set forms. A repeated pitch class in the compositional statement sometimes represents a single instance of that pitch class in the array,

TABLE 9

MODE	KEY	ARRAY		AXIS-INTERVAL 0 CHORDS					AXIS-INTERVAL 5 CHORDS			
0,0	9,9	p_4p_5	(3)	2	2	3			11	5	0	(4)
		p_4p_5		2	2	3			4	0	5	
1,1	8,8	p_4p_5		2	2	3	(1)	(5)	0	4	1	
		i_3i_4		1	2	2			4	11	5	
2,2	7,7	p_4p_5	(2)	3	1	4			0	4	1	(3)
		p_2p_3		1	1	2			3	11	4	
3,3	6,6	p_4p_5		3	1	4	(0)	(4)	1	3	2	
		i_1i_2		0	1	1			3	10	4	
4,4	5,5	p_4p_5	(1)	4	0	5			1	3	2	(2)
		p_0p_1		0	0	1			2	10	3	
5,5	4,4	p_4p_5		4	0	5	(11)	(3)	2	2	3	
		$i_{11}i_0$		11	0	0			2	9	3	
6,6	3,3	p_4p_5	(0)	5	11	6			2	2	3	(1)
		$p_{10}p_{11}$		11	11	0			1	9	2	
7,7	2,2	p_4p_5		5	11	6	(10)	(2)	3	1	4	
		i_9i_{10}		10	11	11			1	8	2	
8,8	1,1	p_4p_5	(11)	6	10	7			3	1	4	(0)
		p_8p_9		10	10	11			0	8	1	
9,9	0,0	p_4p_5		6	10	7	(9)	(1)	4	0	5	
		i_7i_8		9	10	10			0	7	1	
10,10	11,11	p_4p_5	(10)	7	9	8			4	0	5	(11)
		p_6p_7		9	9	10			11	7	0	
11,11	10,10	p_4p_5		7	9	8	(8)	(0)	5	11	6	
		i_5i_6		8	9	9			11	6	0	

(From this point on the above is repeated with the axis-dyad chords at the tritone transposition.)

and vice versa. Any tonic cyclic chord may also be read as a tetrachordal segment of one of the tonic set forms. Overlappings and the pairing of segments of unequal length create still more possibilities for varied readings of the array. Such reinterpretations of identical pitch-class collections open a variety of choices to the composer at every moment in the progress of a composition.

EXAMPLE 37

[cont'd on p. 62]

EXAMPLE 37 [cont'd]

Copyright 1974 by Theodore Presser Co.
Used by permission.

The Toccata commences with three brief thematic ideas (bars 1–3, 4–6, 7–13) that are immediately restated in bars 14–27. The first opens with a tonic chord (A1 and A2) with axis notes *d,d:*

$$p_4p_5: \quad 3 \quad 2 \quad 2$$
$$i_3i_4: \quad\quad 2 \quad 2 \quad 1 \quad (3)$$

There is a literal return of the first thematic idea at bar 14, but the chord into the new array is given one interpretation at B1 and another at B2:

$$p_4p_5: \quad 3 \quad 2 \quad 2 \qquad\qquad p_2p_3: \quad 3 \quad 0 \quad 2 \quad (1)$$
$$p_2p_3: \quad 1 \quad 2 \quad 0 \quad (3) \qquad p_0p_1: \quad 1 \quad 0 \quad 0$$

The second array, p_4p_5/p_2p_3, is thus replaced by its T(11) transposition, p_2p_3/p_0p_1. The second thematic idea remains at T(11) (cf. C1 and C2) through the first half of bar 19. Its initial figure is the same one that opens the work, but the derivation is not analogous. In example 37,b, the axis interval is assumed to be 0 for C1 and C2, as it is for the other chords in the same example. The secondary interval couple of the cyclic chords at C1 and C2 is consequently understood to be 2,2:

$$p_4p_5: \quad 9 \quad 8 \quad 8 \qquad\qquad p_2p_3: \quad 8 \quad 7 \quad 7$$
$$p_2p_3: \quad 7 \quad 8 \quad 6 \quad (9) \qquad p_0p_1: \quad 6 \quad 7 \quad 5 \quad (8)$$

If axis-interval 1 is assumed instead, the secondary interval couple of the cyclic chords will be 11,11, as it is at A1 and A2:

$$p_4p_5: \quad\quad 8 \quad 9 \quad 7 \qquad\qquad p_2p_3: \quad\quad 7 \quad 8 \quad 6$$
$$p_2p_3: \quad (7) \quad 7 \quad 8 \quad 6 \qquad p_0p_1: \quad (6) \quad 6 \quad 7 \quad 5$$

At bars 19–21 the tonic cyclic chord shared by the two arrays returns (cf. D1 and D2):

$$p_4p_5: \quad 9 \quad 8 \quad 8 \qquad\qquad p_2p_3: \quad 9 \quad 6 \quad 8 \quad (7)$$
$$p_2p_3: \quad 7 \quad 8 \quad 6 \quad (9) \qquad p_0p_1: \quad 7 \quad 6 \quad 6$$

This leads into a literal restatement of the first two bars of the third thematic idea. The pivotal cyclic chord in bars 7 and 21 (E1 and E2) may be interpreted as either a component of the third array, p_4p_5/i_1i_2, or a component of its T(1) transposition, p_6p_7/i_3i_4:

$$p_4p_5: \quad 9 \quad 7 \quad 10 \quad (6) \qquad p_6p_7: \quad\quad 9 \quad 9 \quad 10$$
$$i_1i_2: \quad\quad 6 \quad 7 \quad 7 \qquad\qquad i_3i_4: \quad (10) \quad 6 \quad 9 \quad 7$$

The latter interpretation is implied in the continuation of the reprise, where the interval-0 axis note *e* of bar 9 is replaced by *f*$^\sharp$ (bar 23):

p_4p_5: *0   4   1* p_6p_7: *0   6   1*

i_1i_2:   9   4   *10* i_3i_4:   9   6   *10*

The remainder of the reprise is a T(1) transposition of the original passage. A tonic chord concludes the expository statement of the three thematic ideas in bars 1–13 and their first reprise in bars 14–27 (*cf.* F1 and F2):

p_4p_5: 3   *2*   2 p_6p_7: 4   *3*   3

i_1i_2:   0   *2*   11   *(3)* i_3i_4:   1   *3*   0   *(4)*

The new array at bar 28 shares one set form, i_3i_4, with the preceding array, and replaces the other set form of the latter with its cognate, i_5i_6. Thus the set segments that produce the initial axis-dyad chord of the new array,

i_5i_6: 4   2   3   *(3)*

i_3i_4: 2   2   1

may also be interpreted as set segments of the preceding array,

p_6p_7: 3   *4*   2

i_3i_4:   2   2   1   *(3)*

The new array commences with a third statement of the first thematic idea, but this time, in contrast with the literal reprise in bars 14–15, one of the original set forms, p_4p_5, is replaced by its cognate, i_5i_6. The remaining set form, i_3i_4, and *one* of the two cycles of the new set form are compositionally represented exactly as they were at the beginning of the piece, while the pitches derived from the remaining cycle are transposed by T(1). The pitch-class substitution is a minimal one—a semitonal inflection of one pitch class in each sum tetrachord. The qualitative change, however—the replacement of an even axis of symmetry, *d/d* (expressed by p_4), by an odd one, *d/e*$^\flat$ (i_5), and of an odd axis of symmetry, *d/e*$^\flat$ (p_5), by an even one, *e*$^\flat$/*e*$^\flat$ (i_6)—represents the fundamental qualitative distinction in the system: the dichotomy of odd and even dyads that is expressed in the foundational dyadic array on p. 17, above. Analogous set-form alignments of the respective arrays are shown below:

p_4p_5: 3 2 *2 3* 1 *4*   0 5 11 *6* *10* 7   *9 8* 8 *9* 7 *10* 6 11 5 0 4 *1* (3

i_3i_4:   2 2 1 *3* 0 *4* 11 5 *10* 6   9 7   8 8 7 *9* 6 *10* 5 11 4 0 3 *1* (2

i_5i_6: 4 2 3 3 *2 4*   1 5   0 *6* 11 7 *10 8* 9 9 *8 10* 7 11 6 0 5 *1* (4

i_3i_4:   2 2 1 *3* 0 *4* 11 5 *10* 6   9 7   8 8 7 *9* 6 *10* 5 11 4 0 3 *1* (2

17. The Interval-1 and Interval-7 Sets Combined

On p. 54, above, we demonstrated that arrays based on different cycles will generate the same sum tetrachords, changing only the order of these relative to one another. In bars 199–228 of the Toccata each of the set forms of example 37,a, is replaced by an interval-7 set form of the same even sum and of an odd sum at the tritone transposition (Table 10).

TABLE 10

Bars 1–30	Bars 199–228
p_4p_5/i_3i_4	p_4p_{11}/i_9i_4
p_4p_5/p_2p_3	p_4p_{11}/p_2p_9
p_4p_5/i_1i_2	p_4p_{11}/i_7i_2
p_4p_5/i_3i_4	p_4p_{11}/i_9i_4
p_2p_3/p_0p_1	p_2p_9/p_0p_7
p_6p_7/i_3i_4	p_6p_1/i_9i_4
i_5i_6/i_3i_4	$i_{11}i_6/i_9i_4$

The substitution results in the displacement of alternate even adjacencies by their tritone transpositions, as a comparison of the above p_4p_5/i_3i_4 alignment with the following p_4p_{11}/i_9i_4 alignment will show:

p_4p_{11}: 9 *2* 2 9 7 4 0 *11* 5 6 10 *1* 3 8 8 3 1 *10* 6 5 11 *0* 4 7 (9

i_9i_4:   2 2 7 9 0 4 5 *11* 10 6 3 *1* 8 8 1 3 6 *10* 11 5 4 *0* 9 7 (2

This tritone displacement of alternate even adjacencies may be interpreted as referring to interchanges in the respective order positions of these adjacencies. Thus, for example, 1 *3* in i_3i_4 is displaced by 7 *9* in i_9i_4, and 7 *9* in i_3i_4 by 1 *3* in i_9i_4. A comparison of bars 1–2 (ex. 37,a) and 199–200 (ex. 38) will show how the former are converted into the latter through the tritone displacement of selected elements.

EXAMPLE 38

The implications of the order displacements in the conversion from an interval-1 to an interval-7 array are sometimes realized in the composition through rhythmic displacements. Bars 25–26 and 223–224, for example, are identical save for the interchange of the two dyads in the right-hand part (cf. exx. 37,a and 39). The respective sources of the two excerpts in the example are as follows:

p_6p_7:	*11*	7	0		5	*1*	6
i_4i_3:	9	7	8		3	*1*	2

p_6p_1:	*11*	7	6		5	*1*	0
i_9i_4:	9	7	2		3	*1*	8

EXAMPLE 39

A new concept is introduced in the closing bars of the Toccata (ex. 40). Bars 307–312, a final recapitulation of the first thematic idea leading into the coda, are derived from an array in which one of the original interval-1 set forms, i_4i_3, is retained, while the other, p_4p_5, is replaced by an analogous interval-7 set form, $p_{10}p_5$.

EXAMPLE 40

Where in the p_4p_5/i_3i_4 array axis-interval 0 produces cyclic chords of primary intervals 1,1 and secondary intervals 1,1, in the $p_{10}p_5/i_3i_4$ array axis-interval 0 produces cyclic chords of primary intervals 7,1 and secondary intervals 7,1. Cyclic chords that have the same axis dyad in the two arrays will differ only in the tritone transposition of a single pitch class. The interval-0 alignment of the $p_{10}p_5/i_3i_4$ array is shown below. (Two partitions of the alignment are required to generate all the cyclic chords of the given axis interval.)

$p_{10}p_5$: 3 2 8 9 1 4 6 11 11 6 4 1 9 8 2 3 7 10 0 5 5 0 10 7 (3 ‖

i_3i_4:   2 2 1 3 0 4 11 5 10 6 9 7 8 8 7 9 6 10 5 11 4 0 3 1 (2 ‖

0 5 5 0 10 7 3 2 8 9 1 4 6 11 11 6 4 1 9 8 2 3 7 10 (0

11 5 10 6 9 7 8 8 7 9 6 10 5 11 4 0 3 1 2 2 1 3 0 4 (11

The last thematic statement, beginning at bar 307, opens and closes with a chord that is reinterpreted (bar 312) to serve as a link with the new array on which the coda is based:

$p_{10}p_5$:   3   2   8 p_2p_9:   1   1   8

i_3i_4:   2   2   1 i_3i_4:   2   1   3

Each of the remaining axis-interval-0 cyclic chords of the first array will be similarly found in the new array, in association with an axis dyad transposed to T(11):

p_2p_9: 8 1 1 8 6 3 11 10 4 5 9 0 2 7 7 2 0 9 5 4 10 11 3 6 (8 ‖

i_3i_4:   3 1 2 2 1 3 0 4 11 5 10 6 9 7 8 8 7 9 6 10 5 11 4 0 (3 ‖

1 8 6 3 11 10 4 5 9 0 2 7 7 2 0 9 5 4 10 11 3 6 8 1 (1

8 8 7 9 6 10 5 11 4 0 3 1 2 2 1 3 0 4 11 5 10 6 9 7 (8

The axis dyads of the bracketed collections in the example are indicated by their pitch-class numbers. The first two brackets and the last enclose extended segments. In bars 318 and 320f. the axis dyad itself (9,9 in both instances) is omitted. The piece concludes with a simultaneous representation of a cyclic interval, 7, and an adjacency sum, 9. Example 41 shows how the outer voices of the last eleven bars converge upon this point.

EXAMPLE 41

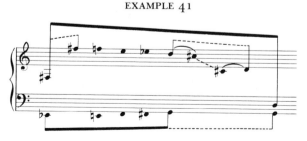

18. Derived Sets

On pp. 33 and 48, above, it was pointed out that **wherever an axis dyad is equivalent to an adjacency of one of the two set forms (of the same cyclic interval) of an array its neighbor notes will form a cyclic chord that duplicates the pitch-class collection of a tetrachordal segment of the other set form of the array. A special function was ascribed to such "tonic" axis dyads and "tonic" cyclic chords. The last three axis dyads of example 40 will each be found as adjacencies, since their sums are respectively 2, 4, and 4, but since the neighbor-note chords each contain two *different* cyclic intervals they cannot be represented as segments of either of the two set forms of the array. They can, however, be represented as segments of "derived" sets generated by both cyclic intervals.** An intervals-1/7 cycle partitions the collection of twelve pitch classes as follows:

$$0 \quad 1 \quad 8 \quad 9 \quad 4 \quad 5 \quad (0$$
$$1 \quad 2 \quad 9 \quad 10 \quad 5 \quad 6 \quad (1$$
$$2 \quad 3 \quad 10 \quad 11 \quad 6 \quad 7 \quad (2$$
$$3 \quad 4 \quad 11 \quad 0 \quad 7 \quad 8 \quad (3$$

From left to right, these represent the partitions of the P cycle; from right to left, the partitions of the I cycle. As P and I cycles they may be combined to produce dyads of a fixed sum. For example:

DYADS OF SUM 3

0 1 8 9 4 5 (0	*1 2 9 10 5 6 (1*	*3 4 11 0 7 8 (3*
3 2 7 6 11 10 (3	2 1 6 5 10 9 (2	0 11 4 3 8 7 (0

Where combined cycles of a single interval were linearized to produce a set, a second adjacency sum was generated, the difference between the two sums being equivalent to the cyclic interval. Where two interval numbers are represented in the cycle, as in this instance, there will be two additional adjacency sums in the linear version of the combined P and I cycles. In the following linearization of the above alignment of intervals-1/7 P and I cycles the brackets mark overlapping tetrachordal segments of i_3i_4 and i_3i_{10}. (The repeated sum within each of these segments will identify the derived set form; the cyclic intervals are shown in parentheses, with the number on the left indicating the cycle of the basic set form of which that sum is a component in the given array, p_2p_9/i_3i_4.)

69

$i_3(1,7)$
```
⌐0  3⌐1  2⌐8  7⌐9  6⌐4  11⌐5  10⌐(0  3⌐   ‖
⌐1  2)⌐2  1⌐9  6⌐10  5⌐(5  10⌐6  9⌐1  2⌐   ‖
⌐3  0⌐4  11)⌐11  4⌐0  3⌐7  8⌐(8  7⌐3  0⌐
```

Our interest lies in the new segments of primary interval couple 1,7 that result from this linearization. The common adjacency sum, 3, will lie at the center of each such segment:

$i_3(1,7)$
```
⌐3  1⌐2  8⌐7  9⌐6  4⌐11  5⌐10  0⌐(3  1⌐   ‖
⌐2)  2⌐1  9⌐6  10⌐5  (5⌐10  6⌐9  1⌐2  2⌐   ‖
⌐0  4⌐11)  11⌐4  0⌐3  7⌐8  (8⌐7  3⌐0  4⌐
```

The above is a tonic derived set form of the p_2p_9/i_3i_4 array on which the concluding bars of example 40 are based. The segments show the tonic cyclic chords that are generated by sum 2 in the following alignment of the array:

p_2p_9:   8 *1* 1 *8* 6 3 11 *10* 4 5 9 0 2 7 7 2   0 9   5 4 10 *11* 3 6 (8 ‖

i_4i_3:   2 1 3 0 4 11 5 10 6 9 7 8 8 7 9 6 *10* 5 *11* 4 0   3 1 2 (2 ‖

1 *8* 6 *3* 11 *10* 4 5 9 0 2 7 7 2 0   9 5   4 10 *11* 3 6 8 *1* (1

9 6 *10* 5 *11*   4 0 3 1 2 2 1 3 0 4 11 5 10   6   9 7 8 8 7 (9

The same alignment gives us another tonic axis dyad, 4, which generates cyclic chords that are represented as segments in the following tonic derived set form:

$p_9(7,1)$
```
⌐3  5⌐4  10⌐11  9⌐0  2⌐7  1⌐8  (6⌐3  5⌐   ‖
⌐4)  4⌐5  9⌐0  8⌐1  (1⌐8  0⌐9  5⌐4  4⌐   ‖
⌐6  2⌐7)  7⌐2  6⌐3  11⌐10  (10⌐11  3⌐6  2⌐
```

The following alignment produces tonic axis dyads of sums 3 and 9:

p_2p_9:   8 *1* 1 *8* 6 3 11 *10*   4 5 9 0 2 7 7 2 0 9 5   4 10 *11* 3 6 (8 ‖

i_4i_3:   7 8 8 7 9 6 *10*   5 *11* 4 0 3 *1* 2 2 *1* 3 0 4 11   5 10 6 9 (7 ‖

1 *8* 6 *3* 11 *10* 4   5 9 0 2 7 7 2 0 9   5 4 10 *11* 3 6 8 *1* (1

2 *1* 3 0   4 11 5 10 6 9 7 8 8 7 9 6 *10* 5 *11*   4 0 3 *1* 2 (2

The tonic cyclic chords generated by sum 3 occur as segments of $p_2(7,1)$, those generated by sum 9 occur as segments of $i_4(1,7)$:

$p_2(7,1)$
$$
\begin{cases}
1 \ 2 \ 0 \ 9 \ 5 \ 10 \ 4 \ 5 \ 9 \ 6 \ 8 \ 1 \ (1 \ 2) \ \| \\
0 \ 3 \ 11 \ 10 \ 4 \ 11 \ 3 \ 6 \ 8 \ 7 \ 7 \ 2 \ (0 \ 3)
\end{cases}
$$

$i_4(1,7)$
$$
\begin{cases}
2 \ 1 \ 3 \ 6 \ 10 \ 5 \ 11 \ 10 \ 6 \ 9 \ 7 \ 2 \ (2 \ 1) \ \| \\
3 \ 0 \ 4 \ 5 \ 11 \ 4 \ 0 \ 9 \ 7 \ 8 \ 8 \ 1 \ (3 \ 0)
\end{cases}
$$

The non-tonic cyclic chords of the p_2p_9/i_3i_4 array, generated by axis dyads of sums other than 2, 4, 3, or 9, occur as segments of "resultant" derived set forms. A T(1) transposition of $i_3(1,7)$ for example,

$i_5(1,7)$
$$
\begin{cases}
4 \ 2 \ 3 \ 9 \ 8 \ 10 \ 7 \ 5 \ 0 \ 6 \ 11 \ 1 \ (4 \ 2) \ \| \\
3) \ 3 \ 2 \ 10 \ 7 \ 11 \ 6 \ (6 \ 11 \ 7 \ 10 \ 2 \ 3 \ 3 \ \| \\
1 \ 5 \ 0) \ 0 \ 5 \ 1 \ 4 \ 8 \ 9 \ (9 \ 8 \ 4 \ 1 \ 5
\end{cases}
$$

represents as segments the cyclic chords of axis-sum 0 (i.e., the complementary transposition, T(11), of the axis dyads of sum 2 whose cyclic chords are represented as segments in $i_3(1,7)$):

p_2p_9:   8 *1*   1 8 6 *3* 11 *10* 4 5 9 0 2   7 7   2 0 9 5 4 10 *11* 3 6   (8

i_4i_3:   *10* 5 *11* 4 0 3   *1*   2 2 1 3 0 4 11 5 10 6 9 7 8   8   7 9 6 (*10*

Each of the above sum alignments of p_2p_9/i_3i_4 produces a repeated series of four sums between vertically aligned pitch classes. In this series the sum of adjacent sums is alternately 0 and 6, i.e., the two sums of the aligned tonic sums, 2+4 and 9+3. The complete sum array from which the above alignments are taken is shown in Table 11.

TABLE 11

p₂p₉: 8 *1* 1 *8* 6 *3* 11 *10*   4 5   9 *0*   2 7   7   2   0   9   5   4 10 *11* 3   6 (8
(3/9/9/3)

i₄i₃: 7   8   *8*   7   *9*   6 *10*   5 *11* 4   0 3   *1* 2   2   1   *3*   0   4 11   5 10 6   9 (7
(8/4/2/10)

p₂p₉: 1 *8*   6 *3* 11 *10*   4   5   9 *0*   2 7   7 2   0   9   5   4 10 *11*   3   6 8 *1* (1
(7/5/1/11)

i₄i₃: *6*   9   7   8   *8*   7   9   6 *10* 5 *11* 4   0 3   *1*   2   2   1   *3*   0   4 11 5 10 (6
(0/0/6/6)

p₂p₉: 6 *3* 11 *10*   4   5   9   0   2 7   7 2   0 9   5   4 10 *11*   3   6   8 *1* 1   8 (6
(11/1/5/7)

i₄i₃: *5* 10   6   9   7   8   *8*   7   9 6 *10* 5 *11* 4   0   *3*   1   2   2   1   *3*   0 4 11 (5
(4/8/10/2)

p₂p₉:11 *10*   4   5   9 *0*   2   7   7 2   0 9   5 4 10 *11*   3   6   8   *1*   1   8 6 *3* (11
(3/9/9/3)

i₄i₃: *4* 11   5 10   6   9   7   8   *8* 7   9 6 *10* 5 *11*   4   0   3   1   2   2   1 *3*   0 (4

19. The Remaining Cyclic Sets

On p. 21, above, we pointed out that an interchange of P and I designations—a mere change in nomenclature—implies a corresponding interchange of complementary cyclic interval numbers. The cyclic set forms of interval 7, interval 3, and interval 1 which have been discussed in the preceding pages are thus respectively equivalent to set forms of the complementary aspect designations and complementary cyclic intervals, 5, 9, and 11.

In example 42 there is a modulation from an interval-3 array, p_6p_9/p_4p_7, to an interval-1 array, i_5i_6/i_3i_4. Each set form of the latter shares a tonic sum with one of the set forms of the former. The modulation is effected by reinterpreting a shared axis-dyad chord so that what are adjacent elements in the interval-3 array become cyclic elements in the interval-1 array:

p_6p_9:	11	7	2	4	5	1	8	10	(11	‖	9)	9	0	6	3	(3	6
p_4p_7:	4	0	7	9	10	6	1	3	(4	‖	2)	2	5	11	8	(8	11

i_6i_5:	3)	3	2	4	1	5	0	6	11	7	10	8	9	(9	8
i_4i_3:	8)	8	7	9	6	10	5	11	4	0	3	1	2	(2	1

A set form of any cyclic interval may be read as a specific partitioning of a member of any other set complex with which it shares an adjacency sum of the same aspect. If we take set forms of interval 1 as source sets, p_6p_9, for example, may be derived from p_6p_7 or p_8p_9 by taking every third adjacency of sum 6 from the former or every third adjacency of sum 9 from the latter:

$$
p_6p_7 \begin{cases} 3,3 & \quad 6,0 & \quad 9,9 & \quad 0,6 & \quad (3,3 \\ \quad 4,2 & \quad 7,11 & \quad 10,8 & \quad 1,5 & \quad (4,2 \\ \quad\quad 5,1 & \quad 8,10 & \quad 11,7 & \quad 2,4 & \quad (5,1 \end{cases}
$$

$$
p_8p_9 \begin{cases} 3,6 & \quad 0,9 & \quad 9,0 & \quad 6,3 & \quad (3,6 \\ \quad 2,7 & \quad 11,10 & \quad 8,1 & \quad 5,4 & \quad (2,7 \\ \quad\quad 1,8 & \quad 10,11 & \quad 7,2 & \quad 4,5 & \quad (1,8 \end{cases}
$$

EXAMPLE 42

Perle, Songs of Praise and Lamentation, III (1974)

Copyright 1975 by Boelke-Bomart, Inc.
Used by permission.

An interval-2 cyclic set form may be analogously derived by taking every second adjacency of a given interval-1 set form. For example:

$$\mathrm{P_6P_7} \begin{cases} 3,3 \quad 5,1 \quad 7,11 \quad\ 9,9 \quad\ 11,7 \quad 1,5 \quad (3,3 \\ \ \ 4,2 \quad 6,0 \quad 8,10 \quad 10,8 \quad\ 0,6 \quad 2,4 \quad (4,2 \end{cases}$$

The alternative dyadic segmentation of the set form thus derived from $\mathrm{P_6P_7}$,

$$3,5 \quad 1,7 \quad 11,9 \quad (9,11 \quad \| \quad 4,4 \quad 2,6 \quad 0,8 \quad 10,10 \quad (8,0$$

partitions a second interval-1 set form as follows:

$$\mathrm{i_8i_7} \begin{cases} 4,4 \quad 2,6 \quad 0,8 \quad 10,10 \quad\ 8,0 \quad 6,2 \quad (4,4 \\ \ \ 3,5 \quad 1,7 \quad 11,9 \quad\ \ 9,11 \quad 7,1 \quad 5,3 \quad (3,5 \end{cases}$$

The given interval-2 set form will show its relationship to the two interval-1 set forms in the name assigned to it, $\mathrm{p_6i_8}$. **Both sums being even, each takes its aspect name from the cycle that contributes the left element of each adjacency** (see p. 21, above). For the adjacencies of sum 6 that element is taken from the P cycle, for the adjacencies of sum 8 it is taken from the I cycle. If the aspect names respectively assigned to the two sums are interchanged ($\mathrm{p_8i_6}$), the same set form is defined as a member of the interval-10 cyclic set complex. **Every set form generated by an even cyclic interval number will similarly consist of alternate adjacency sums of opposite aspect.** For set forms of cyclic-interval 0 or cyclic-interval 6 either cycle of a set form may be defined as P or I without requiring a change in the cyclic interval number, since intervals 0 and 6 are their own mod 12 complements.

20. Alban Berg's Master Array of the Interval Cycles

All twelve interval cycles are combined in the following array (Table 12) in a letter that Berg sent to Schoenberg on July 27, 1920. We have substituted pitch numbers for Berg's conventional notation and interval numbers for his conventional interval names.[22] The respective P and I interval numbers, premised on a reading from left to right, are given at the left of each row. Reading down, one finds the same interval cycles (as indicated by the P and I interval numbers at the head of each column), generated by the differences between the horizontally aligned cycles. We assume that any given cycle may be combined with itself as well as with any other cycle in the array, that the given partition of cycle 0/0, 2/10, 3/9, 4/8, or 6/6 may be replaced by any other partition of the same cycle, and that cycles may be shifted (= transposed) relative to one another like the scales in a slide rule. The array may then be read as an abstract representation of procedures that play a significant and persistent role in Berg's work, from the second song of Opus 2[23] through *Lulu*.

TABLE 12

Cycles P	I	P 0 / I 0	11 / 1	10 / 2	9 / 3	8 / 4	7 / 5	6 / 6	5 / 7	4 / 8	3 / 9	2 / 10	1 / 11	0 / 0
0	0	0	0	0	0	0	0	0	0	0	0	0	0	0
11	1	0	11	10	9	8	7	6	5	4	3	2	1	0
10	2	0	10	8	6	4	2	0	10	8	6	4	2	0
9	3	0	9	6	3	0	9	6	3	0	9	6	3	0
8	4	0	8	4	0	8	4	0	8	4	0	8	4	0
7	5	0	7	2	9	4	11	6	1	8	3	10	5	0
6	6	0	6	0	6	0	6	0	6	0	6	0	6	0
5	7	0	5	10	3	8	1	6	11	4	9	2	7	0
4	8	0	4	8	0	4	8	0	4	8	0	4	8	0
3	9	0	3	6	9	0	3	6	9	0	3	6	9	0
2	10	0	2	4	6	8	10	0	2	4	6	8	10	0
1	11	0	1	2	3	4	5	6	7	8	9	10	11	0
0	0	0	0	0	0	0	0	0	0	0	0	0	0	0

22. A facsimile of Berg's array is found in Perle, "Berg's Master Array of the Interval Cycles," *The Musical Quarterly*, LXIII (1977), p. 5.

23. *Ibid.*, pp. 2f. The reader is referred to the same article for a discussion of Stravinsky's use of interval cycles in *Le Sacre du printemps*. See also Perle, "The Musical Language of *Wozzeck*," *The Music Forum* (Columbia University Press), I (1967), exx. 59, 69, 70.

In the Quartet, Opus 3, for example, there are numerous passages which are direct statements of, or reducible to, segments of various cyclic alignments. Often Berg employs these segments much as a tonal composer might use scale or arpeggio figures to fill in registral or durational space. Example 43, for instance, is derivable from the following alignment of P-4 and P-5 interval cycles. The difference between the two cyclic intervals, 1 or 11, determines the series of vertical intervals produced by the alignment.

P-4:	7	11	3	7	11	3	7	11	3	7	11	3	(7
P-5:	9	2	7	0	5	10	3	8	1	6	11	4	(9
Intervals:	10	9	8	7	6	5	4	3	2	1	0	11	(10

EXAMPLE 43

II, 153   Berg, Op. 3

Combined interval cycles also serve to outline extended progressions. The following cyclical progression may be abstracted from bars 24–28 of the second movement (ex. 44).

EXAMPLE 44

In pitch-class number notation we may read this as an alignment of three P cycles:

P-1:	–	–	8	9	10	11
P-7:	7	2	9	4	11	6
P-7:	1	8	3	10	5	0

A principal thematic idea of the first movement (ex. 45) is derived from an I-1 and I-5 alignment. Adjacent vertical intervals produced by the paired cycles show the same difference as the respective cyclic intervals ($1-5=8$, or $5-1=4$):

I-1:	8	7	6	5	4	3	2	1	0	11	10	9	(8
I-5:	5	0	7	2	9	4	11	6	1	8	3	10	(5
Intervals:	3	7	11	3	7	11	3	7	11	3	7	11	(3

EXAMPLE 45

Copyright 1925 by Universal Edition, A.G., Vienna.
Renewed 1953 by Helene Berg.
Used by permission.

When the same thematic idea returns at the conclusion of the movement an I-2 cycle is joined to the original I-1 and I-5 cycles (ex. 46):

I-1:	8	7	6	.	.	.
I-2:	5	3	1	.	.	.
I-5:	5	0	7	.	.	.

EXAMPLE 46

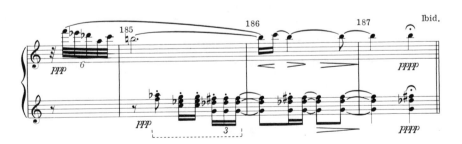

At bars 13–19 of the second movement equivalent and non-equivalent opposite cycles are aligned between first violin and cello (ex. 47). It will be recalled that paired opposite cycles have been characterized by the *sums* produced by their vertical dyads. Adjacent vertical sums will show the same difference as the respective cyclic intervals.

P-5:			P-1:						
10	3	8	1	2	3	4	5	6	7
2	1	0	11	10	9	8	6	4	2

I-1:   I-2:

Sums:	0	4	8	0	0	0	0	11	10	9

EXAMPLE 47

21. Sum and Difference Scales

In example 48 we show, in conventional notation, slide-rule representations of the sum-7 and sum-9 columns of the table of dyadic sums and differences on page 17. Opposite cycles of interval 2 are represented if we read every second dyad, opposite cycles of interval 3 if we read every third, and so on.

EXAMPLE 48

By similarly converting all the columns of the table into such equivalently calibrated sum scales, each on a separate strip, we can conveniently perform operations such as are described in Chapter 14 and translate the given slide-rule settings into musical notation. The three settings in number notation on page 54, for example—respectively based on cycles of interval 7, interval 1, and interval 2, may all be read from the alignment of the two pitch scales as given in example 48. The same series of sum tetrachords may be derived from an alignment of two sum-8 scales (ex. 49).

EXAMPLE 49

Each row of the table of dyadic sums and differences may be similarly converted into conventionally notated difference scales. The following alignment of such scales gives us a third reading of the same series of sum tetrachords (ex. 50).

EXAMPLE 50

All the pitch-class relations which are the subject of the present study may be directly derived from and demonstrated by means of such sum-scale and difference-scale alignments. In the following pages all arrays are derived by means of slide-rule operations employing the rows and columns of the basic dyadic array as difference scales and sum scales respectively.

22. The Master Modes

Since all cyclic set forms may be derived by partitioning set forms of interval 1, the latter may serve as source sets for all arrays. We will take for illustration the i_6i_5/i_4i_3 alignment given on page 73, above. From this we may derive two difference scales, one showing the paired I cycles of the two set forms, the other their paired P cycles. The two difference scales are aligned to produce a tetrachord of primary-sums 6 and 4, secondary-sums 11 and 11, in each column, with the components of the first and fourth rows taken from one of the two set forms, and the components of the second and third rows taken from the other:

Diff. 7:
3	2	1	0	11	10	9	8	7	6	5	4	(3
8	7	6	5	4	3	2	1	0	11	10	9	(8

Diff. 5:
8	9	10	11	0	1	2	3	4	5	6	7	(8
3	4	5	6	7	8	9	10	11	0	1	2	(3

If we read down successive columns, this setting of the two difference scales gives us the intervals-7/5 alignment of i_6i_5/i_4i_3 (= the cyclic intervals 11,11 array, p_6p_5/p_4p_3). Consecutive alternate columns of the same setting produce the 7/5 alignment of the cyclic intervals 2,2 array, i_6p_4/i_4p_2 (= the 10,10 array, p_6i_4/p_4i_2):

i_6p_4: 3) *3 1 5 11 7 9* (9 7 | 2 4 0 6 10 8 (8 *10*

i_4p_2: 8) *8 6 10 4 0 2* (2 0 | 7 9 5 *11* 3 *1* (1 *3*

Reading every third column we similarly derive the 7/5 alignment of the cyclic intervals 3,3 array, i_6i_3/i_4i_1 (= the 9,9 array, p_6p_3/p_4p_1):

i_6i_3: 3) *3 0 6 9* (9 6 | 2 4 11 7 8 *10* 5 *1* (2 *4*

i_4i_1: 8) *8 5 11 2* (2 11 | 7 *9* 4 *0* 1 *3* 10 6 (7 *9*

Every fourth column taken consecutively produces the 7/5 alignment of the cyclic intervals 4,4 array, i_6p_2/i_4p_0 (= the 8,8 array, p_6i_2/p_4i_0), and so on for the cyclic intervals 5,5 array, i_6i_1/i_4i_{11} (= the 7,7 array, p_6p_1/p_4p_{11}), and the cyclic intervals 6,6 array, which may be read as either i_6p_0/i_4p_{10} or p_6i_0/p_4i_{10} since interval 6 is its own complement. We continue with the cyclic intervals 7,7 array i_6i_{11}/i_4i_9 (= the 5,5 array, p_6p_{11}/p_4p_9), the 8,8 array, i_6p_{10}/i_4p_8 (= the 4,4 array, p_6i_{10}/p_4i_8) and so on. In the cyclic intervals 0,0 array, i_6p_6/i_4p_4, each column of the paired difference scales forms a separate partition:

i_6p_6:   3) *3*   (3 | 2   4   (2 *4* | 1   5   (1 *5* | . . .

i_4p_4:   8) *8*   (8 | 7   9   (7 *9* | 6   10   (6 *10* | . . .

The same arrays in their complementary sequence are produced when the two difference scales are interchanged:

Diff. 5:	8	9	10	11	0	1	2	3	4	5	6	7	(8
	3	4	5	6	7	8	9	10	11	0	1	2	(3

Diff. 7:	3	2	1	0	11	10	9	8	7	6	5	4	(3
	8	7	6	5	4	3	2	1	0	11	10	9	(8

The same reading that previously gave us i_6i_5/i_4i_3 now produces the sum-10 complementary array, p_4p_5/p_6p_7.[24] Similarly, i_6p_4/i_4p_2 is replaced by p_4i_6/p_6i_8, i_6i_3/i_4i_1 by p_4p_7/p_6p_9, i_6p_2/i_4p_0 by p_4i_8/p_6i_{10}, and so on.

A change in the alignment of the two difference scales will replace the original tetrachord of primary-sums 6 and 4 by another whose primary sums will show the same difference. For example, a shift of difference-scale 7 one degree to the left substitutes 5 and 3 for the original primary sums:

Diff. 7:	2	1	0	11	10	9	8	7	6	5	4	3	(2
	7	6	5	4	3	2	1	0	11	10	9	8	(7

Diff. 5:	8	9	10	11	0	1	2	3	4	5	6	7	(8
	3	4	5	6	7	8	9	10	11	0	1	2	(3

The secondary sum couple is similarly converted from 11,11 to 10,10. The interval couple of each tetrachord remains 7,5, since it is represented by the same difference scales. From the new setting of these scales we derive the intervals-7/5 alignments of p_5p_4/p_3p_2, p_5i_3/p_3i_1, p_5p_2/p_3p_0, etc.

The addition of a third scale enlarges each column to include the cyclic interval, so that a complete axis-dyad chord is represented in each column (Table 13).

TABLE 13

Diff. 5:	7	8	9	10	11	0	1	2	3	4	5	6	(7
	2	3	4	5	6	7	8	9	10	11	0	1	(2

Diff. 7:	3	2	1	0	11	10	9	8	7	6	5	4	(3
	8	7	6	5	4	3	2	1	0	11	10	9	(8

Diff. 5:	8	9	10	11	0	1	2	3	4	5	6	7	(8
	3	4	5	6	7	8	9	10	11	0	1	2	(3

24. **The sum of complementation here refers to complementary adjacency sums, not to the sum of complementary pitch classes of the respective set forms; i.e., each tonic sum of the former array subtracted from 10 gives us a tonic sum of opposite aspect in a set form of the same cyclic interval in the latter array. The sum of complementation of pitch classes of the respective set forms will be 10 %. 2, or (12+10) %. 2.**

Corresponding elements of the two difference-5 scales produce the cyclic intervals, 1,1 (or 11,11). Each column now shows an axis dyad of interval 7 and its two neighbor-note dyads in i_6i_5/i_4i_3, one of the two arrays on which example 42 is based. The setting of difference scales in Table 14 produces the chords of axis-interval 5 in the other array of example 42, p_6p_9/p_4p_7.

TABLE 14

Diff. 7:	6	5	4	3	2	1	0	11	10	9	8	7	(6
	11	10	9	8	7	6	5	4	3	2	1	0	(11
Diff. 5:	*8*	*9*	*10*	*11*	*0*	*1*	*2*	*3*	*4*	*5*	*6*	*7*	*(8*
	3	*4*	*5*	*6*	*7*	*8*	*9*	*10*	*11*	*0*	*1*	*2*	*(3*
Diff. 7:	3	2	1	0	11	10	9	8	7	6	5	4	(3
	8	7	6	5	4	3	2	1	0	11	10	9	(8

Intersecting axis-dyad chords of the two arrays occur in the respective third columns and (at the tritone transposition) the respective ninth columns of the two difference-scale alignments.

All the axis-dyad chords of the intervals-7/5 alignment of i_6i_5/i_4i_3, as well as its two types of sum tetrachords (of primary-sums 6 and 4 and primary-sums 5 and 3), may be read as segments of columns in Table 15.

TABLE 15

Diff. 5:	*7*	*8*	*9*	*10*	*11*	*0*	*1*	*2*	*3*	*4*	*5*	*6*	*(7*
	2	*3*	*4*	*5*	*6*	*7*	*8*	*9*	*10*	*11*	*0*	*1*	*(2*
Diff. 7:	3	2	1	0	11	10	9	8	7	6	5	4	(3
	8	7	6	5	4	3	2	1	0	11	10	9	(8
Diff. 5:	*8*	*9*	*10*	*11*	*0*	*1*	*2*	*3*	*4*	*5*	*6*	*7*	*(8*
	3	*4*	*5*	*6*	*7*	*8*	*9*	*10*	*11*	*0*	*1*	*2*	*(3*
Diff. 7:	2	1	0	11	10	9	8	7	6	5	4	3	(2
	7	6	5	4	3	2	1	0	11	10	9	8	(7

A shift in the position of one of the scales in Table 15 will generate a new cyclic interval. This will require a corresponding shift in the position of one of the scales that represents the opposite pair of cycles, to produce a complementary revision in the cyclic interval generated by the latter. In Table 16, for example, i_6i_5 is replaced by i_6p_4 and i_4i_3 by i_4p_2, the new set forms representing cyclic-intervals 2,2.

TABLE 16

Diff. 5:	6	7	8	9	10	11	0	1	2	3	4	5	(6
	1	2	3	4	5	6	7	8	9	10	11	0	(1

Diff. 7:	3	2	1	0	11	10	9	8	7	6	5	4	(3
	8	7	6	5	4	3	2	1	0	11	10	9	(8

Diff. 5:	8	9	10	11	0	1	2	3	4	5	6	7	(8
	3	4	5	6	7	8	9	10	11	0	1	2	(3

Diff. 7:	1	0	11	10	9	8	7	6	5	4	3	2	(1
	6	5	4	3	2	1	0	11	10	9	8	7	(6

The conversion of the i_6i_5/i_4i_3 setting (Table 15) illustrated in Table 17 replaces the respective set forms by i_8i_5/i_6i_3.

TABLE 17

Diff. 5:	7	8	9	10	11	0	1	2	3	4	5	6	(7
	2	3	4	5	6	7	8	9	10	11	0	1	(2

Diff. 7:	3	2	1	0	11	10	9	8	7	6	5	4	(3
	8	7	6	5	4	3	2	1	0	11	10	9	(8

Diff. 5:	10	11	0	1	2	3	4	5	6	7	8	9	(10
	5	6	7	8	9	10	11	0	1	2	3	4	(5

Diff. 7:	0	11	10	9	8	7	6	5	4	3	2	1	(0
	5	4	3	2	1	0	11	10	9	8	7	6	(5

If alternate scales—scales representing the same cycles—are equally shifted in the same direction, the cyclic interval will remain constant. For each such change in the alignment of difference scales a corresponding change will affect each of the original adjacency sums. In the series of difference-scale settings illustrated in Table 18 the primary interval couple throughout is 1,1, but each time the difference-5 scales are shifted by one place to the left the adjacency sums are increased by 1. The mode throughout is 2,2, and the key is revised by the addition of 2,2 for successive arrays.

In combination, the various procedures described above will generate every Mode 2,2 (= 10,10) array of every cyclic interval system in which that mode can be represented. (Both set forms of the array will necessarily share the same cyclic interval.) Since we have operated exclusively with difference scales of 7 and 5, only the intervals-7/5 alignments of the arrays have been represented. The alignments of Mode 2,2 would entail seven pairs of difference scales, each such pair showing a difference of 2 between the interval numbers represented by its scales (cf. the Mode 2,2 array on p. 44, above): 1/11 (= 11/1), 2/0 (= 10/0), 3/1 (= 9/11), 4/2 (= 8/10), 5/3 (= 7/9), 6/4 (= 6/8), 7/5 (= 5/7). The 3/1 alignment of i_6i_5/i_4i_3 is shown below (Table 19).

TABLE 18

Key 9,9 i_3i_4/i_5i_6					Key 11,11 p_4p_5/p_6p_7					Key 1,1 i_5i_6/i_7i_8					Key 3,3 p_6p_7/p_8p_9				
7	8	9	.	.	8	9	10	.	.	9	10	11	.	.	10	11	0	.	.
2	3	4	.	.	3	4	5	.	.	4	5	6	.	.	5	6	7	.	.
3	2	1	.	.	3	2	1	.	.	3	2	1	.	.	3	2	1	.	.
8	7	6	.	.	8	7	6	.	.	8	7	6	.	.	8	7	6	.	.
8	9	10	.	.	9	10	11	.	.	10	11	0	.	.	11	0	1	.	.
3	4	5	.	.	4	5	6	.	.	5	6	7	.	.	6	7	8	.	.
2	1	0	.	.	2	1	0	.	.	2	1	0	.	.	2	1	0	.	.
7	6	5	.	.	7	6	5	.	.	7	6	5	.	.	7	6	5	.	.

TABLE 19

Diff. 1:	5	6	7	8	9	10	11	0	1	2	3	4	(5
	4	5	6	7	8	9	10	11	0	1	2	3	(4
Diff. 3:	1	0	11	10	9	8	7	6	5	4	3	2	(1
	10	9	8	7	6	5	4	3	2	1	0	11	(10
Diff. 1:	6	7	8	9	10	11	0	1	2	3	4	5	(6
	5	6	7	8	9	10	11	0	1	2	3	4	(5
Diff. 3:	0	11	10	9	8	7	6	5	4	3	2	1	(0
	9	8	7	6	5	4	3	2	1	0	11	10	(9

The remaining modes may be analogously derived by pairing P and I difference scales whose difference numbers are separated by the interval numbers that characterize the mode. Thus the replacement, in the preceding setting of difference scales, of the P scale of difference 1 by the P scale of difference 6 produces a Mode 9,9 array. The setting of difference scales in Table 20, for example, gives us the 3/6 alignment of p_0p_1/i_3i_4.

TABLE 20

Diff. 6:	5	6	7	8	9	10	11	0	1	2	3	4	(5
	11	0	1	2	3	4	5	6	7	8	9	10	(11
Diff. 3:	1	0	11	10	9	8	7	6	5	4	3	2	(1
	10	9	8	7	6	5	4	3	2	1	0	11	(10
Diff. 6:	6	7	8	9	10	11	0	1	2	3	4	5	(6
	0	1	2	3	4	5	6	7	8	9	10	11	(0
Diff. 3:	0	11	10	9	8	7	6	5	4	3	2	1	(0
	9	8	7	6	5	4	3	2	1	0	11	10	(9

Among all these various realignments and interchanges of difference scales, for any combination of such scales alternate scales have so far been of identical difference number and aspect. In consequence, the cycles of both set forms of each array have been generated by the same interval. **All the scale settings described in the preceding paragraphs are segments of a single "master mode" which, because it comprises *all* difference arrays whose paired set forms are of the *same* cyclic interval, we will call "Master Mode O."**

On p. 68, above, we show a difference alignment of set-forms p_2p_9/i_3i_4. These belong to two different set complexes, of cyclic-intervals 7 and 1. Where a single recurrent vertical interval is produced when cycles of the same aspect and interval number are paired, alternate vertical intervals whose difference is 6 are produced where the respective intervals of the paired cycles are 7 and 1 or any other numbers of the same difference. In the alignment of 7 and 1 cycles of p_2p_9/i_3i_4 on p. 68 the paired I cycles alternately produce vertical intervals 5 and 11, the paired P cycles alternately produce vertical intervals 0 and 6. There is thus a recurring series of four vertical intervals, 5/0/11/6, rather than two as in the arrays of Master Mode 0. The following setting of difference scales (Table 21) unfolds, in successive alternate columns, both partitions of the given alignment of p_2p_9/i_3i_4. **The array is a member of Master Mode 6, since alternate difference scales show a difference of 6.** The first two scales are repeated in order to complete the cyclic chords of axis-interval 5.

TABLE 21

Diff. 5:	8	7	6	5	4	3	2	1	0	11	10	9	(8
	3	2	1	0	11	10	9	8	7	6	5	4	(3

Diff. 0:	*1*	*2*	*3*	*4*	*5*	*6*	*7*	*8*	*9*	*10*	*11*	*0*	*(1*
	1	*2*	*3*	*4*	*5*	*6*	*7*	*8*	*9*	*10*	*11*	*0*	*(1*

Diff. 11:	*1*	*0*	*11*	*10*	*9*	*8*	*7*	*6*	*5*	*4*	*3*	*2*	*(1*
	2	*1*	*0*	*11*	*10*	*9*	*8*	*7*	*6*	*5*	*4*	*3*	*(2*

Diff. 6:	*2*	*3*	*4*	*5*	*6*	*7*	*8*	*9*	*10*	*11*	*0*	*1*	*(2*
	8	*9*	*10*	*11*	*0*	*1*	*2*	*3*	*4*	*5*	*6*	*7*	*(8*

Diff. 5:	6	5	4	3	2	1	0	11	10	9	8	7	(6
	1	0	11	10	9	8	7	6	5	4	3	2	(1

Diff. 0:	*3*	*4*	*5*	*6*	*7*	*8*	*9*	*10*	*11*	*0*	*1*	*2*	*(3*
	3	*4*	*5*	*6*	*7*	*8*	*9*	*10*	*11*	*0*	*1*	*2*	*(3*

The complete representation of p_2p_9/i_3i_4 through difference-scale settings requires three partitions of the latter: 0/11/6/5 (= 0/1/6/7), 4/3/10/9 (= 8/9/2/3), 8/7/2/1 (= 4/5/10/11). The secondary intervals of the cyclic chord of axis-interval 0 show the mode of the array (i.e., the differences between the aligned adjacency sums of the paired set forms). All Mode

11,5 or 1,7 arrays[25] may be represented as the various settings of these same groups of difference scales. The same procedures for the conversion of difference-scale settings that were applied to the arrays of Master Mode 0 will apply to Master Mode 6 and all other master modes.

An inspection of example 51 shows it to consist of a series of axis-dyad chords, with each note in the left hand representing an axis dyad of interval 0 and the four 32nd-notes on the same beat representing a corresponding cyclic chord.

EXAMPLE 51

Lansky, Modal Fantasy (1970)

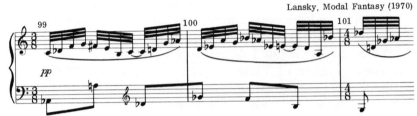

Copyright 1975 by Columbia University Press.
Galaxy Music Corporation, sole agent.
Used by permission.

The respective cyclic chords form sums of 8, 9, 1, and 3 with their axis notes, and may thus be derived in any array whose two set forms are generated by adjacencies of these sums. If, for example, we assume that one of the two set forms of the array is p_8p_9, the other will be either i_1p_3 or i_3p_1, depending on whether the cyclic interval chosen for the second set form is 2 or 10. Though i_1p_3 and i_3p_1 are equivalent set forms, the two arrays, p_8p_9/i_1p_3 and p_8p_9/i_3p_1, are not equivalent. (We substitute the mod 12 complement of the cyclic interval for only *one* of the two set forms, not for both, since the latter substitution would amount to a change in nomenclature only: i_9i_8/i_3p_1 is the same array as p_8p_9/i_1p_3.) P_8p_9/i_1p_3 is an array of Master Mode 1, p_8p_9/i_3p_1 an array of Master Mode 3.[26] A tetrachordal segmentation of the former joins sum 8 with sum 1 and sum 9 with sum 3, whereas a tetrachordal segmentation of the latter joins sum 8 with sum 3 and sum 9 with sum 1. The respective axis-dyad

25. **Whether we classify p_2p_9/i_3i_4 as a Mode 11,5 or 1,7 array depends on whether we determine the differences between the aligned adjacency sums by subtracting the adjacency sums of i_3i_4 from those of p_2p_9 or vice versa.** (Cf. p. 29, above.) **Arrays in the same interval system and of the same or complementary modal designations, regardless of whether or not they are transposable and/or invertible into one another, may all be said to belong to the same modal class,** or modal type, and will be found in tables of the same series of difference-scale numbers.

26. **Master modes and master keys (see below) are assigned the number of the lesser difference between cyclic intervals.** Thus $2-1(=1)$ gives us the number of the master mode in which p_8p_9/i_1p_3 is found, rather than $1-2(=11)$.

chords in the two arrays are identical as to pitch-class content but they occur in a different order. **We will call arrays so related, where one of the two set forms of the one array is replaced by the equivalent set form of the complementary cyclic interval in the other array, "semi-equivalent."**

A complete representation of p_8p_9/i_1p_3 by means of difference scales, as of any other Master Mode 1 array, brings all twelve P scales and all twelve I scales together in a single table. The last two scales in Table 22, 9 and 2, are respectively equivalent to the scales of the complementary interval numbers, 3 and 10. A continuation similarly repeats the preceding scales, substituting the complementary difference number for each.

The difference-scale representation of the semi-equivalent array, p_8p_9/i_3p_1, falls into two partitions (Table 23).

Another array that can serve as the source of example 51 is p_8p_3/i_1p_9. Since this is in the same mode (7,6) as p_8p_9/i_1p_3, it may be represented by the same series of difference scales as the latter, with alternate adjacent pairs of scales shifted by six places to right or left to show the new cyclic intervals (Table 24). Both arrays will comprise the same collections of sum tetrachords, since in both sum 8 is aligned with sum 1, sum 9 with sum 3. In each column the paired alternate dyads that form cyclic chords from equivalent difference scales of the two arrays will be identical as to interval but not pitch content, since one of the dyads will always be the tritone transposition of the corresponding dyad of the other array. Two exceptions occur, where one of the neighbor-note dyads is interval 6. Around axis-interval 1 the neighbor-note dyads are identical where the respective axis dyads are a tritone apart, and around axis-interval 0 the complete series of axis-dyad chords are identical in the two arrays. The replacement of one of the two set forms of p_8p_3/i_1p_9 by the equivalent set form of the complementary cyclic interval will, as before, repeat the same collection of axis-dyad chords in a new order and context.

A third and final pair of semi-equivalent arrays from which we may derive the axis-dyad chords of example 51 is p_8p_1/i_9p_3 and p_8p_1/i_3p_9. Where one of the two set forms of an array has 6 or 0 as its cyclic interval the substitution of either set form by the equivalent set form of the complementary cyclic interval will not change the master mode to which the array belongs. The semi-equivalent arrays p_8p_1/i_9p_3 and p_8p_1/i_3p_9 are both members of Master Mode 1, but in other respects the distinctions between sets so related hold.

The information contained in example 51 is insufficient to define the array more explicitly than we have indicated in the preceding paragraphs. The six arrays intersect where difference-scale 0 and its two neighboring scales appear, and no axis-dyad chords other than these are

TABLE 22

Diff. 4:	*1*	*2*	*3*	*4*	*5*	*6*	*7*	*8*	*9*	*10*	*11*	*0*	*(1*
	9	10	11	0	1	2	3	4	5	6	7	8	(9
Diff. 9:	4	3	2	1	0	11	10	9	8	7	6	5	(4
	7	6	5	4	3	2	1	0	11	10	9	8	(7
Diff. 3:	*2*	*3*	*4*	*5*	*6*	*7*	*8*	*9*	*10*	*11*	*0*	*1*	*(2*
	11	0	1	2	3	4	5	6	7	8	9	10	(11
Diff. 8:	2	1	0	11	10	9	8	7	6	5	4	3	(2
	6	5	4	3	2	1	0	11	10	9	8	7	(6
Diff. 2:	*3*	*4*	*5*	*6*	*7*	*8*	*9*	*10*	*11*	*0*	*1*	*2*	*(3*
	1	2	3	4	5	6	7	8	9	10	11	0	(1
Diff. 7:	0	11	10	9	8	7	6	5	4	3	2	1	(0
	5	4	3	2	1	0	11	10	9	8	7	6	(5
Diff. 1:	*4*	*5*	*6*	*7*	*8*	*9*	*10*	*11*	*0*	*1*	*2*	*3*	*(4*
	3	*4*	*5*	*6*	*7*	*8*	*9*	*10*	*11*	*0*	*1*	*2*	*(3*
Diff. 6:	10	9	8	7	6	5	4	3	2	1	0	11	(10
	4	3	2	1	0	11	10	9	8	7	6	5	(4
Diff. 0:	*5*	*6*	*7*	*8*	*9*	*10*	*11*	*0*	*1*	*2*	*3*	*4*	*(5*
	5	*6*	*7*	*8*	*9*	*10*	*11*	*0*	*1*	*2*	*3*	*4*	*(5*
Diff. 5:	8	7	6	5	4	3	2	1	0	11	10	9	(8
	3	2	1	0	11	10	9	8	7	6	5	4	(3
Diff. 11:	*6*	*7*	*8*	*9*	*10*	*11*	*0*	*1*	*2*	*3*	*4*	*5*	*(6*
	7	8	9	10	11	0	1	2	3	4	5	6	(7
Diff. 4:	6	5	4	3	2	1	0	11	10	9	8	7	(6
	2	1	0	11	10	9	8	7	6	5	4	3	(2
Diff. 10:	7	8	9	10	11	0	1	2	3	4	5	6	(7
	9	10	11	0	1	2	3	4	5	6	7	8	(9
Diff. 3:	4	3	2	1	0	11	10	9	8	7	6	5	(4
	1	0	11	10	9	8	7	6	5	4	3	2	(1
Diff. 9:	*8*	*9*	*10*	*11*	*0*	*1*	*2*	*3*	*4*	*5*	*6*	*7*	*(8*
	11	0	1	2	3	4	5	6	7	8	9	10	(11
Diff. 2:	2	1	0	11	10	9	8	7	6	5	4	3	(2
	0	11	10	9	8	7	6	5	4	3	2	1	(0

TABLE 23

Diff. 7:	4	5	6	7	8	9	10	11	0	1	2	3	(4
	9	10	11	0	1	2	3	4	5	6	7	8	(9
Diff. 2:	6	5	4	3	2	1	0	11	10	9	8	7	(6
	4	3	2	1	0	11	10	9	8	7	6	5	(4
Diff. 10:	5	6	7	8	9	10	11	0	1	2	3	4	(5
	7	8	9	10	11	0	1	2	3	4	5	6	(7
Diff. 5:	8	7	6	5	4	3	2	1	0	11	10	9	(8
	3	2	1	0	11	10	9	8	7	6	5	4	(3
Diff. 1:	6	7	8	9	10	11	0	1	2	3	4	5	(6
	5	6	7	8	9	10	11	0	1	2	3	4	(5
Diff. 8:	10	9	8	7	6	5	4	3	2	1	0	11	(10
	2	1	0	11	10	9	8	7	6	5	4	3	(2
Diff. 4:	7	8	9	10	11	0	1	2	3	4	5	6	(7
	3	4	5	6	7	8	9	10	11	0	1	2	(3
Diff. 11:	0	11	10	9	8	7	6	5	4	3	2	1	(0
	1	0	11	10	9	8	7	6	5	4	3	2	(1
Diff. 3:	2	3	4	5	6	7	8	9	10	11	0	1	(2
	11	0	1	2	3	4	5	6	7	8	9	10	(11
Diff. 10:	4	3	2	1	0	11	10	9	8	7	6	5	(4
	6	5	4	3	2	1	0	11	10	9	8	7	(6
Diff. 6:	3	4	5	6	7	8	9	10	11	0	1	2	(3
	9	10	11	0	1	2	3	4	5	6	7	8	(9
Diff. 1:	6	5	4	3	2	1	0	11	10	9	8	7	(6
	5	4	3	2	1	0	11	10	9	8	7	6	(5
Diff. 9:	4	5	6	7	8	9	10	11	0	1	2	3	(4
	7	8	9	10	11	0	1	2	3	4	5	6	(7
Diff. 4:	8	7	6	5	4	3	2	1	0	11	10	9	(8
	4	3	2	1	0	11	10	9	8	7	6	5	(4
Diff. 0:	5	6	7	8	9	10	11	0	1	2	3	4	(5
	5	6	7	8	9	10	11	0	1	2	3	4	(5
Diff. 7:	10	9	8	7	6	5	4	3	2	1	0	11	(10
	3	2	1	0	11	10	9	8	7	6	5	4	(3
Diff. 3:	6	7	8	9	10	11	0	1	2	3	4	5	(6
	3	4	5	6	7	8	9	10	11	0	1	2	(3
Diff. 10:	0	11	10	9	8	7	6	5	4	3	2	1	(0
	2	1	0	11	10	9	8	7	6	5	4	3	(2

TABLE 24

Diff.													
Diff. 4:	1	2	3	4	5	6	7	8	9	10	11	0	(1
	9	10	11	0	1	2	3	4	5	6	7	8	(9
Diff. 9:	4	3	2	1	0	11	10	9	8	7	6	5	(4
	7	6	5	4	3	2	1	0	11	10	9	8	(7
Diff. 3:	8	9	10	11	0	1	2	3	4	5	6	7	(8
	5	6	7	8	9	10	11	0	1	2	3	4	(5
Diff. 8:	8	7	6	5	4	3	2	1	0	11	10	9	(8
	0	11	10	9	8	7	6	5	4	3	2	1	(0
Diff. 2:	3	4	5	6	7	8	9	10	11	0	1	2	(3
	1	2	3	4	5	6	7	8	9	10	11	0	(1
Diff. 7:	0	11	10	9	8	7	6	5	4	3	2	1	(0
	5	4	3	2	1	0	11	10	9	8	7	6	(5
Diff. 1:	10	11	0	1	2	3	4	5	6	7	8	9	(10
	9	10	11	0	1	2	3	4	5	6	7	8	(9
Diff. 6:	4	3	2	1	0	11	10	9	8	7	6	5	(4
	10	9	8	7	6	5	4	3	2	1	0	11	(10
Diff. 0:	5	6	7	8	9	10	11	0	1	2	3	4	(5
	5	6	7	8	9	10	11	0	1	2	3	4	(5
Diff. 5:	8	7	6	5	4	3	2	1	0	11	10	9	(8
	3	2	1	0	11	10	9	8	7	6	5	4	(3
Diff. 11:	0	1	2	3	4	5	6	7	8	9	10	11	(0
	1	2	3	4	5	6	7	8	9	10	11	0	(1
Diff. 4:	0	11	10	9	8	7	6	5	4	3	2	1	(0
	8	7	6	5	4	3	2	1	0	11	10	9	(8
Diff. 10:	7	8	9	10	11	0	1	2	3	4	5	6	(7
	9	10	11	0	1	2	3	4	5	6	7	8	(9
Diff. 3:	4	3	2	1	0	11	10	9	8	7	6	5	(4
	1	0	11	10	9	8	7	6	5	4	3	2	(1
Diff. 9:	2	3	4	5	6	7	8	9	10	11	0	1	(2
	5	6	7	8	9	10	11	0	1	2	3	4	(5
Diff. 2:	8	7	6	5	4	3	2	1	0	11	10	9	(8
	6	5	4	3	2	1	0	11	10	9	8	7	(6

given in the example. As we pointed out above, semi-equivalent arrays contain the same axis-dyad chords, but not the same sum tetrachords. The latter means of differentiating between semi-equivalent arrays are not provided in the quoted excerpt of the composition.

A paraphrase of example 51 occurs a few bars later (ex. 52). In searching for the source of this new passage we note that three of the previous sums, 8, 9, and 1, are retained, and the fourth sum, 3, is replaced by 11. The three pairs of semi-equivalent arrays that will generate the axis-dyad chords in example 52 are $p_8p_9/i_{11}p_1$ and p_8p_9/i_1p_{11}, p_8p_{11}/i_9p_1 and p_8p_{11}/i_1p_9, $p_8p_1/i_{11}p_9$ and p_8p_1/i_9p_{11}. The first repeats the primary interval couples (1,2 and 1,10) of one of the three pairs of semi-equivalent arrays inferred from the preceding example (p_8p_9/i_1p_3 and p_8p_9/i_3p_1). Alternate difference scales, since they determine the cyclic intervals, remain intact relative to one another between arrays that share primary interval couples, as a comparison of the difference-scale representation of p_8p_9/i_1p_3 (Table 22) with the following difference-scale representation of $p_8p_9/i_{11}p_1$ (Table 25) will show.

EXAMPLE 52

Assuming that we wish to give preference to the most economical interpretation of the two passages together, we would hypothesize their respective derivation from arrays that are most simply converted into one another. We would then consider, in addition to the above mentioned arrays of identical cyclic intervals, arrays of the same mode: p_8p_1/i_9p_3 for example 51 and p_8p_{11}/i_9p_1 for example 52, both of which are in Mode 11,10; and p_8p_3/i_9p_1 for example 51 and p_8p_1/i_9p_{11} for example 52, both of which are in Mode 11,2.

TABLE 25

Diff.	0	1	2	3	4	5	6	7	8	9	10	11	
Diff. 5:	0	1	2	3	4	5	6	7	8	9	10	11	(0
	7	8	9	10	11	0	1	2	3	4	5	6	(7
Diff. 8:	4	3	2	1	0	11	10	9	8	7	6	5	(4
	8	7	6	5	4	3	2	1	0	11	10	9	(8
Diff. 4:	1	2	3	4	5	6	7	8	9	10	11	0	(1
	9	10	11	0	1	2	3	4	5	6	7	8	(9
Diff. 7:	2	1	0	11	10	9	8	7	6	5	4	3	(2
	7	6	5	4	3	2	1	0	11	10	9	8	(7
Diff. 3:	2	3	4	5	6	7	8	9	10	11	0	1	(2
	11	0	1	2	3	4	5	6	7	8	9	10	(11
Diff. 6:	0	11	10	9	8	7	6	5	4	3	2	1	(0
	6	5	4	3	2	1	0	11	10	9	8	7	(6
Diff. 2:	3	4	5	6	7	8	9	10	11	0	1	2	(3
	1	2	3	4	5	6	7	8	9	10	11	0	(1
Diff. 5:	10	9	8	7	6	5	4	3	2	1	0	11	(10
	5	4	3	2	1	0	11	10	9	8	7	6	(5
Diff. 1:	4	5	6	7	8	9	10	11	0	1	2	3	(4
	3	4	5	6	7	8	9	10	11	0	1	2	(3
Diff. 4:	8	7	6	5	4	3	2	1	0	11	10	9	(8
	4	3	2	1	0	11	10	9	8	7	6	5	(4
Diff. 0:	5	6	7	8	9	10	11	0	1	2	3	4	(5
	5	6	7	8	9	10	11	0	1	2	3	4	(5
Diff. 3:	6	5	4	3	2	1	0	11	10	9	8	7	(6
	3	2	1	0	11	10	9	8	7	6	5	4	(3
Diff. 11:	6	7	8	9	10	11	0	1	2	3	4	5	(6
	7	8	9	10	11	0	1	2	3	4	5	6	(7
Diff. 2:	4	3	2	1	0	11	10	9	8	7	6	5	(4
	2	1	0	11	10	9	8	7	6	5	4	3	(2
Diff. 10:	7	8	9	10	11	0	1	2	3	4	5	6	(7
	9	10	11	0	1	2	3	4	5	6	7	8	(9
Diff. 1:	2	1	0	11	10	9	8	7	6	5	4	3	(2
	1	0	11	10	9	8	7	6	5	4	3	2	(1

23. The Master Keys

Just as we can represent difference arrays by tables of difference scales, so can we represent sum arrays by tables of sum scales. Where each difference scale of the master mode comprises two interval-1 cycles of identical aspect, each sum scale of the "master key" will comprise two interval-1 cycles of opposite aspect. We return, for illustrative purposes, to the i_5i_6/i_3i_4 array whose intervals-7/5 alignment was converted into difference scales on pp. 82ff., above. The following realignment of the two set forms produces alternate sums of 10 and 11 where the earlier version (p. 73) produced alternate differences of 7 and 5:

i_5i_6: *2 3 3 2 4 1 5 0 6 11 7 10 8 9 9 8 10 7 11 6 0 5 1 4 (2*

i_4i_3: *8 8 7 9 6 10 5 11 4 0 3 1 2 2 1 3 0 4 11 5 10 6 9 7 (8*

From this we derive scales of sums 10 and 11 and align them to produce a tetrachord of sums 5 and 4 in each column, with the components of the first and fourth rows (respectively, P and I cycles) taken from one of the two set forms and the components of the second and third rows (respectively I and P columns) taken from the other:

Sum 10:
2	*3*	*4*	*5*	*6*	*7*	*8*	*9*	*10*	*11*	*0*	*1*	*(2*
8	7	6	5	4	3	2	1	0	11	10	9	(8

Sum 11:
8	*9*	*10*	*11*	*0*	*1*	*2*	*3*	*4*	*5*	*6*	*7*	*(8*
3	2	1	0	11	10	9	8	7	6	5	4	(3

If we read down successive columns, this setting of the two sum scales gives us the sums-10/11 alignment of i_5i_6/i_3i_4.[27] Consecutive alternate columns of the same setting produce the two partitions of the 10/11 alignment of the cyclic-intervals 2,2 array, i_5p_7/p_2i_4:

i_5p_7: *2 3 4 1 6 11 8 9 10 7 0 5 (2* ‖

i_4p_2: *8 8 6 10 4 0 2 2 0 4 10 6 (8* ‖

 3 2 5 0 7 10 9 8 11 6 1 4 (3

 7 9 5 11 3 1 1 3 11 5 9 7 (7

---

27. **In the names of arrays, correspondingly placed numbers of the two set forms show the paired adjacencies for modes, and oppositely placed numbers show the paired adjacencies for keys. Thus the mode of the i_5i_6/i_3i_4 array is 2,2 (=5−3, 6−4), and its key is 9,9 (=5+4, 3+6).** Where paired adjacencies of a mode have the same aspect

Reading every third column we similarly derive the 10/11 alignment of the cyclic-intervals 3,3 array, i_5i_8/i_1i_4. Every fourth column taken consecutively produces the 10/11 alignment of the cyclic-intervals 4,4 array, i_5p_9/p_0i_4, every fifth column the 10/11 alignment of the cyclic-intervals 5,5 array, $i_5i_{10}/i_{11}i_4$, and so on. Where the analogous readings of paired difference scales produced a series of arrays that showed a progressive change of key but preserved the same mode, paired sum scales produce a series of arrays that show a progressive change of mode but preserve the same key. An interchange of the two sum scales will produce the same series of arrays, merely reversing their order.

An inversional complement of the above setting of sum-scales 10 and 11 will be found by subtracting each pitch-class number of that setting from a given sum of complementation. Suppose we assume the latter to be 11. The P-1 cycle of sum-scale 10 will be replaced by an I-1 cycle: 9 8 7...; the I-1 cycle of sum-scale 10 will be replaced by a P-1 cycle: *3 4 5*.... Since the P and I cycles of sum-scale 11 are already inversionally related at sum 11, no change is necessary here.

Sum 0:	*3*	*4*	*5*	*6*	*7*	*8*	*9*	*10*	*11*	*0*	*1*	*2*	*(3*
	9	8	7	6	5	4	3	2	1	0	11	10	(9

Sum 11:	*8*	*9*	*10*	*11*	*0*	*1*	*2*	*3*	*4*	*5*	*6*	*7*	*(8*
	3	2	1	0	11	10	9	8	7	6	5	4	(3

From the principle of tritone equivalence we can infer that the same sum-scale setting is generated where the sum of complementation of each pitch-class number is assumed to be 11+6(=5). The paired sum scales shifted six degrees to the left will show the respective sum-5 complements of the given setting of sum-scales 10 and 11:

Sum 0:	*9*	*10*	*11*	*0*	*1*	*2*	*3*	*4*	*5*	*6*	*7*	*8*	*(9*
	3	2	1	0	11	10	9	8	7	6	5	4	(3

Sum 11:	*2*	*3*	*4*	*5*	*6*	*7*	*8*	*9*	*10*	*11*	*0*	*1*	*(2*
	9	8	7	6	5	4	3	2	1	0	11	10	(9

The new sum-scale numbers are found by subtracting each of the original sum-scale numbers from 11+11(=10) or 5+5, i.e., the combined sums of complementation of each pair of P and I cycles. The same operation applied to the adjacency sums that identified the original array, i_5i_6/i_3i_4, and the substitution of the complementary aspect designations, give us the name of the new array, p_5p_4/p_7p_6, that will be found by reading down successive columns of the above setting of sum-scales 0 and 11.

---

name (i.e., where both are p or both are i), both will be even or both will be odd, and where they have opposite aspect names one will be even and the other odd; the opposite is true for keys.

Consecutive alternate columns will similarly produce the complement, p_5i_3/i_8p_6, of the earlier array of cyclic-intervals 2,2 (i_5p_7/p_2i_4). The earlier array of cyclic-intervals 3,3 (i_5i_8/i_1i_4) is analogously replaced by p_5p_2/p_9p_6, the earlier array of cyclic-intervals 4,4 (i_5p_9/p_0i_4) by $p_5i_1/i_{10}p_6$, and so on.

All the axis-dyad chords of the sums-10/11 alignment of i_5i_6/i_3i_4, as well as its two types of sum tetrachords (of primary-sums 3 and 6 and primary-sums 5 and 4), may be read as segments of columns in Table 26.

TABLE 26

Sum 11:	7	8	9	10	11	0	1	2	3	4	5	6	(7
	4	3	2	1	0	11	10	9	8	7	6	5	(4

Sum 10:	2	3	4	5	6	7	8	9	10	11	0	1	(2
	8	7	6	5	4	3	2	1	0	11	10	9	(8

Sum 11:	8	9	10	11	0	1	2	3	4	5	6	7	(8
	3	2	1	0	11	10	9	8	7	6	5	4	(3

Sum 10:	3	4	5	6	7	8	9	10	11	0	1	2	(3
	7	6	5	4	3	2	1	0	11	10	9	8	(7

A shift in the position of one of the scales in the above setting will generate new cyclic intervals. If the third scale, for example, is shifted one degree to the left, the cyclic intervals generated by the two scales of sum 11 are changed from 1,1 to 2,2. A corresponding change is then required in the relation between the other two scales, to produce a complementary revision in the alternate cyclic intervals. For example, the second scale may be shifted one degree to the right. The paired set forms generated by the new alignment are

$$p_4i_6: \quad 7 \quad 9 \quad 9 \quad 7 \quad 11 \quad 5 \quad . \quad . \quad .$$

$$p_5i_3: \quad 4 \quad 1 \quad 2 \quad 3 \quad 0 \quad 5 \quad . \quad . \quad .$$

If the selected corresponding change is, instead, that of the fourth scale one degree to the left, the following paired set forms are generated:

$$i_3p_5: \quad 7 \quad 8 \quad 9 \quad 6 \quad 11 \quad 4 \quad . \quad . \quad .$$

$$i_6p_4: \quad 4 \quad 2 \quad 2 \quad 4 \quad 0 \quad 6 \quad . \quad . \quad .$$

The selected corresponding change may affect the second and fourth scales simultaneously. Suppose, for example, that the second scale is shifted three degrees to the left. The fourth scale must then be shifted four degrees to the left, to produce the following paired set forms:

$$p_0i_2: \quad 7 \quad 5 \quad 9 \quad 3 \quad 11 \quad 1 \quad . \quad . \quad .$$

$$p_9i_7: \quad 4 \quad 5 \quad 2 \quad 7 \quad 0 \quad 9 \quad . \quad . \quad .$$

In every case the combined adjacency sums, i.e., the key, will be 9,9.

If alternate scales are equally shifted, so that the relations between adjacent scales are equivalently altered, the cyclic interval remains constant and for each change in the alignment of sum scales a constant corresponding to that change affects each of the original adjacency sums. In the series of sum-scale settings illustrated in Table 27, for example, the primary intervals throughout are 1,1, the key throughout is 9,9, and the mode is revised by the subtraction of 2,2 for successive arrays.

TABLE 27

Mode 2,2 i_5i_6/i_3i_4				Mode 0,0 p_4p_5/p_4p_5				Mode 10,10 i_3i_4/i_5i_6				Mode 8,8 p_2p_3/p_6p_7			
7	8	9	. .	8	9	10	. .	9	10	11	. .	10	11	0	. .
4	3	2	. .	3	2	1	. .	2	1	0	. .	1	0	11	. .
2	3	4	. .	2	3	4	. .	2	3	4	. .	2	3	4	. .
8	7	6	. .	8	7	6	. .	8	7	6	. .	8	7	6	. .
8	9	10	. .	9	10	11	. .	10	11	0	. .	11	0	1	. .
3	2	1	. .	2	1	0	. .	1	0	11	. .	0	11	10	. .
3	4	5	. .	3	4	5	. .	3	4	5	. .	3	4	5	. .
7	6	5	. .	7	6	5	. .	7	6	5	. .	7	6	5	. .

Table 28 shows the 4/5 alignment of i_5i_6/i_3i_4. Since axis-dyad sums 4 and 5 are tonic adjacencies, their neighbor-note chords are tonic chords, i.e., tetrachordal segments of i_5i_6 and i_3i_4 respectively:

i_5i_6: 4 1 ⌐ 5 0 ⌐ 6 11 ⌐ 7 10 ⌐ 8 9 ⌐ 9 8 ⌐ 10 7 ⌐ 11 6 ⌐ 0 5 ⌐ 1 4 ⌐ 2 3 ⌐ 3 2 (4

i_4i_3: 0 4 ⌐ 11 5 ⌐ 10 6 ⌐ 9 7 ⌐ 8 8 ⌐ 7 9 ⌐ 6 10 ⌐ 5 11 ⌐ 4 0 ⌐ 3 1 ⌐ 2 2 ⌐ 1 3 (0

TABLE 28

Sum 5:	4	5	6	7	8	9	10	11	0	1	2	3 (4
	1	0	11	10	9	8	7	6	5	4	3	2 (1
Sum 4:	5	6	7	8	9	10	11	0	1	2	3	4 (5
	11	10	9	8	7	6	5	4	3	2	1	0 (11
Sum 5:	5	6	7	8	9	10	11	0	1	2	3	4 (5
	0	11	10	9	8	7	6	5	4	3	2	1 (0
Sum 4:	6	7	8	9	10	11	0	1	2	3	4	5 (6
	10	9	8	7	6	5	4	3	2	1	0	11 (10

Our earlier table of sum-scales 10 and 11 for the same array (Table 26) similarly produces, as cyclic chords around axis dyads of sums 10 and 11 respectively, the tetrachordal segments of *resultant* set forms, $i_{11}i_0$ and i_9i_{10}:

$i_{11}i_0$: ⌐7 4 ⌐8 3⌐⌐9 2⌐⌐10 1⌐⌐⌐11 0⌐⌐0 11⌐⌐⌐1 10⌐⌐2 9⌐⌐3 8⌐⌐4 7⌐⌐5 6⌐⌐6 5⌐ (7

$i_{10}i_9$: ⌐9 *1* ⌐8 2⌐⌐7 3⌐⌐6 4⌐⌐5 5⌐⌐4 6⌐⌐3 7⌐⌐2 8⌐⌐1 9⌐⌐0 10⌐⌐11 *11*⌐ 10 0⌐ (9

Examples 27 and 31 illustrate the tonic segmentation if i_9i_4 and p_0p_7 produced by neighbor-note chords of axis dyads of sums 0 and 4. The sum-scale representation of both examples is shown in Table 29.

TABLE 29

Sum 4:	*9*	*10*	*11*	*0*	*1*	*2*	*3*	*4*	*5*	*6*	*7*	*8* (9
	7	6	5	4	3	2	1	0	11	10	9	8 (7
Sum 0:	*0*	*1*	*2*	*3*	*4*	*5*	*6*	*7*	*8*	*9*	*10*	*11* (0
	0	11	10	9	8	7	6	5	4	3	2	1 (0
Sum 4:	*4*	*5*	*6*	*7*	*8*	*9*	*10*	*11*	*0*	*1*	*2*	*3* (4
	0	11	10	9	8	7	6	5	4	3	2	1 (0
Sum 0:	*7*	*8*	*9*	*10*	*11*	*0*	*1*	*2*	*3*	*4*	*5*	*6* (7
	5	4	3	2	1	0	11	10	9	8	7	6 (5

Alternate scales of the preceding sum arrays have the same sum, which means that both set forms of any one of these arrays are generated by the same cyclic interval. All of these sum arrays are segments of a single "Master Key" which we call "Master Key 0." We will refer to "Master Mode 0" and "Master Key 0" collectively as "Master Array 0." A sum alignment of the array discussed on pp. 69ff., above, whose two set forms are respectively generated by cyclic-intervals 7 and 1, will show alternate sums that differ by 6 for each pair of aligned cycles. The array is therefore a member of Master Key 6. The complete p_2p_9/i_3i_4 sum array (p. 72, above) may be represented by means of sum scales (Table 30). The neighbor-note chords of axis dyads of the tonic sums will be equivalent to tetrachordal segments of *tonic* derived set forms, and all other neighbor-note chords will be equivalent to tetrachordal segments of *resultant* derived set forms (cf. pp. 69–72, above). The secondary sums of the neighbor-note chords are 4 and 10 for axis-dyad sum 2; 8 and 2 for axis-dyad sum 4; 3 and 9 for axis-dyad sums 3 and 9. These are the sum couples produced by adjacencies in the tetrachordal segments of the tonic derived set forms of cyclic-intervals 1,7 that were illustrated above (pp. 70f.) in connection with the p_2p_9/i_3i_4 array.

In Table 30, for example, if we take every eighth column (8 being the sum of the cyclic intervals, 1 and 7) of sum-scales 8 and 2, we unfold a partition of the tonic derived set $p_9(7,1)$; if we take the aligned eighth columns of sum-scales 4 and 10 we unfold a partition of the tonic derived set $i_3(1,7)$. (Cf. Tables 30 and 31. It will be recalled that the number on the left of the two cyclic-interval numbers shown in parentheses indicates the cycle of the basic set forms, p_2p_9 and i_3i_4, from which the respective tonic sums of the derived sets, p_9 and i_3, are taken. Subtracting each of the cyclic-interval numbers from 9, since this is an odd sum in its p aspect, we find the secondary-sums 8 and 2, of the cyclic chord. Adding each of the cyclic-interval numbers to 3, since this is an odd sum in its i aspect, we find the secondary sums, 4 and 10, of the cyclic chord.)

Partitions of the other two tonic derived set forms are similarly derived (Table 32). (For $p_2(7,1)$, since the tonic sum is even and in its p aspect, we add the cyclic intervals to that sum to find the secondary sums, 3 and 9, of the cyclic chord. For $i_4(1,7)$, since the tonic sum is even and in its i aspect, we subtract the cyclic intervals from that sum to find the secondary sums, 3 and 9, of the cyclic chord.)

The resultant derived set forms of the array are found by taking complementary transpositions of $p_9(7,1)$ and $i_3(1,7)$ (p_{11} and i_1, p_1 and i_{11}, p_3 and i_9, p_5 and i_7, and p_7 and i_5), and complementary transpositions of $p_2(7,1)$ and $i_4(1,7)$ (p_4 and i_2, p_6 and i_0, p_8 and i_{10}, p_{10} and i_8, and p_0 and i_6). The non-tonic axis-dyad sums 6 and 0 (Table 33), for example, unfold resultant derived set forms $p_7(7,1)$ and $i_5(1,7)$.

TABLE 30

Sum 3:	7	8	9	10	11	0	1	2	3	4	5	6	(7
	8	7	6	5	4	3	2	1	0	11	10	9	(8
Sum 9:	1	2	3	4	5	6	7	8	9	10	11	0	(1
	8	7	6	5	4	3	2	1	0	11	10	9	(8
Sum 9:	8	9	10	11	0	1	2	3	4	5	6	7	(8
	1	0	11	10	9	8	7	6	5	4	3	2	(1
Sum 3:	8	9	10	11	0	1	2	3	4	5	6	7	(8
	7	6	5	4	3	2	1	0	11	10	9	8	(7
Sum 3:	9	10	11	0	1	2	3	4	5	6	7	8	(9
	6	5	4	3	2	1	0	11	10	9	8	7	(6
Sum 8:	7	8	9	10	11	0	1	2	3	4	5	6	(7
	1	0	11	10	9	8	7	6	5	4	3	2	(1
Sum 4:	8	9	10	11	0	1	2	3	4	5	6	7	(8
	8	7	6	5	4	3	2	1	0	11	10	9	(8
Sum 2:	8	9	10	11	0	1	2	3	4	5	6	7	(8
	6	5	4	3	2	1	0	11	10	9	8	7	(6
Sum 10:	3	4	5	6	7	8	9	10	11	0	1	2	(3
	7	6	5	4	3	2	1	0	11	10	9	8	(7
Sum 8:	9	10	11	0	1	2	3	4	5	6	7	8	(9
	11	10	9	8	7	6	5	4	3	2	1	0	(11
Sum 4:	10	11	0	1	2	3	4	5	6	7	8	9	(10
	6	5	4	3	2	1	0	11	10	9	8	7	(6
Sum 7:	6	7	8	9	10	11	0	1	2	3	4	5	(6
	1	0	11	10	9	8	7	6	5	4	3	2	(1
Sum 5:	8	9	10	11	0	1	2	3	4	5	6	7	(8
	9	8	7	6	5	4	3	2	1	0	11	10	(9
Sum 1:	7	8	9	10	11	0	1	2	3	4	5	6	(7
	6	5	4	3	2	1	0	11	10	9	8	7	(6
Sum 11:	3	4	5	6	7	8	9	10	11	0	1	2	(3
	8	7	6	5	4	3	2	1	0	11	10	9	(8
Sum 7:	8	9	10	11	0	1	2	3	4	5	6	7	(8
	11	10	9	8	7	6	5	4	3	2	1	0	(11
Sum 5:	10	11	0	1	2	3	4	5	6	7	8	9	(10
	7	6	5	4	3	2	1	0	11	10	9	8	(7

[cont'd on p. 102]

Sum 0:	6	7	8	9	10	11	0	1	2	3	4	5	(6
	6	5	4	3	2	1	0	11	10	9	8	7	(6
Sum 0:	3	4	5	6	7	8	9	10	11	0	1	2	(3
	9	8	7	6	5	4	3	2	1	0	11	10	(9
Sum 6:	7	8	9	10	11	0	1	2	3	4	5	6	(7
	11	10	9	8	7	6	5	4	3	2	1	0	(11
Sum 6:	10	11	0	1	2	3	4	5	6	7	8	9	(10
	8	7	6	5	4	3	2	1	0	11	10	9	(8
Sum 0:	8	9	10	11	0	1	2	3	4	5	6	7	(8
	4	3	2	1	0	11	10	9	8	7	6	5	(4

TABLE 31

Sum 8:	7	3	11	(7
	1	5	9	(1
Sum 4:	8	4	0	(8
	8	0	4	(8
Sum 2:	8	4	0	(8
	6	10	2	(6
Sum 10:	3	11	7	(3
	7	11	3	(7

$p_9(7,1)$: ⌐7 1 8 6⌐3 5 4 10⌐11 9 0 2⌐ (7

$i_3(1,7)$: 7) 8 8 7 3⌐0 4 11 11⌐4 0 3 7⌐

Axis-dyad sums: 4 2   4 2   4 2

TABLE 32

Sum 9:
$$\begin{array}{ccc} 1 & 9 & 5 & (1 \\ 8 & 0 & 4 & (8 \end{array}$$

Sum 9:
$$\begin{array}{ccc} 8 & 4 & 0 & (8 \\ 1 & 5 & 9 & (1 \end{array}$$

Sum 3:
$$\begin{array}{ccc} 8 & 4 & 0 & (8 \\ 7 & 11 & 3 & (7 \end{array}$$

Sum 3:
$$\begin{array}{ccc} 9 & 5 & 1 & (9 \\ 6 & 10 & 2 & (6 \end{array}$$

$p_2(7,1)$: 1) ⌐1 8 6 9¬⌐5 4 10 5¬⌐9 0 2 1¬

$i_4(1,7)$: ⌐1 8 8 7¬⌐9 0 4 11¬ ⌐5 4 0 3¬ (1

Axis-dyad sums: 9 3   9 3   9 3

TABLE 33

Sum 6:
$$\begin{array}{ccc} 6 & 2 & 10 & (6 \\ 0 & 4 & 8 & (0 \end{array}$$

Sum 6:
$$\begin{array}{ccc} 9 & 5 & 1 & (9 \\ 9 & 1 & 5 & (9 \end{array}$$

Sum 0:
$$\begin{array}{ccc} 7 & 3 & 11 & (7 \\ 5 & 9 & 1 & (5 \end{array}$$

Sum 0:
$$\begin{array}{ccc} 4 & 0 & 8 & (4 \\ 8 & 0 & 4 & (8 \end{array}$$

$p_7(7,1)$: ⌐6 0 7 5¬⌐2 4 3 9¬⌐10 8 11 1¬ (6

$i_5(1,7)$: 8) ⌐9 9 8 4¬⌐1 5 0 0¬ ⌐5 1 4 8¬

Example 53 is based on a Master Key 1 array ($p_{10}i_0/i_9i_{10}$) (Table 34).

TABLE 34

Sum 5:	7	8	9	10	11	0	1	2	3	4	5	6	(7
	10	9	8	7	6	5	4	3	2	1	0	11	(10
Sum 4:	2	3	4	5	6	7	8	9	10	11	0	1	(2
	2	1	0	11	10	9	8	7	6	5	4	3	(2
Sum 4:	8	9	10	11	0	1	2	3	4	5	6	7	(8
	8	7	6	5	4	3	2	1	0	11	10	9	(8
Sum 5:	4	5	6	7	8	9	10	11	0	1	2	3	(4
	1	0	11	10	9	8	7	6	5	4	3	2	(1
Sum 3:	9	10	11	0	1	2	3	4	5	6	7	8	(9
	6	5	4	3	2	1	0	11	10	9	8	7	(6
Sum 6:	6	7	8	9	10	11	0	1	2	3	4	5	(6
	0	11	10	9	8	7	6	5	4	3	2	1	(0
Sum 2:	10	11	0	1	2	3	4	5	6	7	8	9	(10
	4	3	2	1	0	11	10	9	8	7	6	5	(4
Sum 7:	8	9	10	11	0	1	2	3	4	5	6	7	(8
	11	10	9	8	7	6	5	4	3	2	1	0	(11
Sum 1:	11	0	1	2	3	4	5	6	7	8	9	10	(11
	2	1	0	11	10	9	8	7	6	5	4	3	(2
Sum 8:	10	11	0	1	2	3	4	5	6	7	8	9	(10
	10	9	8	7	6	5	4	3	2	1	0	11	(10
Sum 0:	0	1	2	3	4	5	6	7	8	9	10	11	(0
	0	11	10	9	8	7	6	5	4	3	2	1	(0
Sum 9:	0	1	2	3	4	5	6	7	8	9	10	11	(0
	9	8	7	6	5	4	3	2	1	0	11	10	(9
Sum 11:	1	2	3	4	5	6	7	8	9	10	11	0	(1
	10	9	8	7	6	5	4	3	2	1	0	11	(10
Sum 10:	2	3	4	5	6	7	8	9	10	11	0	1	(2
	8	7	6	5	4	3	2	1	0	11	10	9	(8
Sum 10:	2	3	4	5	6	7	8	9	10	11	0	1	(2
	8	7	6	5	4	3	2	1	0	11	10	9	(8
Sum 11:	4	5	6	7	8	9	10	11	0	1	2	3	(4
	7	6	5	4	3	2	1	0	11	10	9	8	(7

EXAMPLE 53

Perle, Seventh Quartet, I (1973)

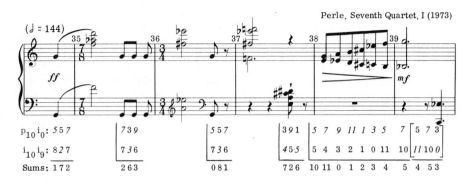

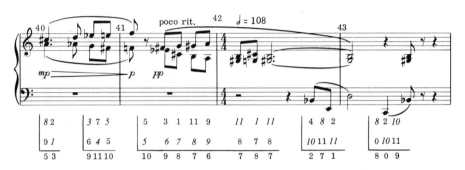

Copyright 1977 by Boelke-Bomart, Inc.
Used by permission.

We have seen that the compositional realization of an array may often be equally well interpreted in terms of either sum or difference scales. The passage quoted in example 53, however, clearly gives priority to the sum version of $p_{10}i_0/i_9i_{10}$. The first two axis-dyad chords unfold five-note segments of the two set forms in an unambiguous sum alignment:[28]

$$
\begin{array}{lccccc}
p_{10}i_0: & 5 & 5 & 7 & 3 & 9 \\
i_{10}i_9: & 8 & 2 & 7 & 3 & 6 \\
\hline
\text{Sums:} & 1 & 7 & 2 & 6 & 3
\end{array}
$$

The third and fourth axis-dyad chords are an equally unambiguous statement of the following segment of the sum array:

28. When the order of the scales in a table is reversed, so that columns are read upwards rather than downwards, the P and I attributions to the cycles are interchanged.

$p_{10}i_0$: ⌐5 5 7¬⌐3 9 1¬

$i_{10}i_9$:   7 *3* 6 *4* 5 *5*

Sums: 0 8 1 7 2 6

In the next bar an interval-2 P cycle is aligned with an interval-1 I cycle, an alignment which, by definition, can only occur in a sum array. The note *f*, sustained through bar 37, is the point of origin of the progression. Interpreting this note, at the end of bar 37, as a doubling and thus as a representation of sum 10, we can read it from either sum-10 scale where these scales intersect in the table. The combined dyads 5,5 and 7,4 of sums 10 and 11 may be read as a sum tetrachord of primary sum-couple 0,9 or as a cyclic chord of primary interval-couple 2,1. The latter reading initiates a cyclic progression to the point of intersection of the two sum-4 scales, where we find another pair of dyads, 5,11 and 7,10 (of sums 4 and 5), which may be read as part of the cyclic progression (primary interval-couple 2,1) or as a sum tetrachord (primary sum-couple 0,9). The series of sum-10 dyads in mm. 40–41 may be interpreted as a segment of one of the two tonic set forms, i_9i_{10}:

9 *1* 8 *2* 7 *3* 6 *4* 5 *5*

or as a representation of paired p_{10} and i_{10} adjacencies, as in the analysis given in the example. In m. 41 the doubled *f* again initiates a cyclic progression, consisting this time, to the end of the bar, of an interval-1 P cycle and an interval-2 I cycle. The last two axis-dyad chords are the only part of the example that may reasonably be referred to the difference array:

$p_{10}i_0$: ⌐4   8   2¬ 10

i_9i_{10}:   11 *11* 10   0

Intervals: 5   3   4   2

24. Composing with Sum Tetrachords

A sum tetrachord in itself gives us very little information about the array from which it is derived. The cyclic intervals are not represented at all; one of the three sum couples of the tetrachord will represent two of the four adjacency sums of the array, but the tetrachord in itself gives no special priority to this primary sum couple. Looking only at the third simultaneity in example 54, for instance, and reading it as a sum tetrachord, all we can deduce is that it is derived from an array whose two set forms may be respectively segmented into adjacencies of sums 0 and 5, or 8 and 9, or 2 and 3. Since the alternative dyadic segmentation of the respective set forms is not implied, we can come to no conclusion as to their aspect or cyclic interval.

EXAMPLE 54

Perle, Sonnets to Orpheus, No. 2 (1974)

Copyright 1975 by Boelke-Bomart, Inc.
Used by permission.

Where we have several sum tetrachords, however, it is usually not difficult to deduce the array. Three of the chords in the example (A, B, and E) are each divisible into dyads whose combined sum is 12. We can assume that the primary sum couple is 2,10, since this is the only sum couple that the three tetrachords have in common. Chords C and F are each divisible into dyads whose combined sum is 5. The only sum couple they share is 2,3. We know, therefore, that adjacencies of sum 2 may be aligned with adjacencies of either 10 or 3, from which we conclude that one of the two set forms of the array is $p_{10}p_3$ or its equivalent, i_3i_{10}, the choice of name depending on whether the cyclic interval is defined as 5 or 7.

Chords D and H are each divisible into dyads whose combined sum is 3. They share two sum couples, 5,10 and 7,8. Since we already know that 10 is one of the tonic sums, we conclude that the primary sum couple shared by D and H is 5,10. The second set form of the array is therefore p_2p_5 or its equivalent, i_5i_2, depending on whether we choose to define the cyclic interval as 3 or 9. (The eight tetrachords of example 54 are analyzed into their primary sum couples in example 55. The slurs embrace continuous segments of the respective set forms.)

EXAMPLE 55

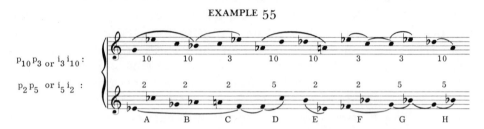

The array, then, is either $p_{10}p_3/p_2p_5$ (= i_3i_{10}/i_5i_2) or $p_{10}p_3/i_5i_2$ (= i_3i_{10}/p_2p_5). What we read as differences (i.e., representations of the mode) in either one of these two semi-equivalent arrays will be read as sums (i.e., representations of the key) in the other.

Example 56, like example 54, consists entirely of sum tetrachords, each except the last divisible into dyads whose combined sum is 7. Chords A through G hold two sum couples in common, 3,4 and 9,10. The dyads that produce the third, variable, sum represent the different transpositions of an invariant interval couple, 5,6 (or 7,6). Chords G through J likewise share two sum couples, 3,4 and 0,7, and an interval couple, 3,4 (or 9,8). The final chord, divisible into dyads whose combined sum is 3, has 4,11 as one of its sum couples. Sum 4 is thus represented by a dyad in every chord in the example, in combination with either 3 or 11. We are therefore able to identify, on the basis of the common dyadic sum content of the different chords, one of the two set forms of the array as i_3p_{11} or $i_{11}p_3$, and one of the two adjacency sums (4) of the other set form.

EXAMPLE 56

Perle, Sonnets to Orpheus, No. 3 (1974)

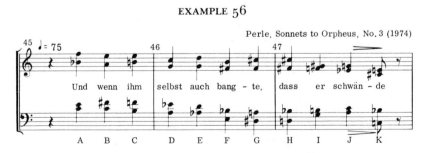

Copyright 1975 by Boelke-Bomart, Inc.
Used by permission.

If we derive the first ten chords from a sum version of the array, the last chord will be found in the difference version of the same array, and vice versa. The paired sum scales 9 and 10 produce chords A through G, and the paired sum scales 7 and 0 produce chords G through J, when the respective sum scales are aligned so as to produce the primary sum couple, 3,4:

Sum 9:	*4*	*5*	*6*	*7*	*8*	*9*	*10*	*11*	*0*	*1*	*2*	*3*	*(4*
	5	4	3	2	1	0	11	10	9	8	7	6	(5
	A	C				D	F		B		E	G	(A
Sum 10:	*10*	*11*	*0*	*1*	*2*	*3*	*4*	*5*	*6*	*7*	*8*	*9*	*(10*
	0	11	10	9	8	7	6	5	4	3	2	1	(0

Sum 7:	*1*	*2*	*3*	*4*	*5*	*6*	*7*	*8*	*9*	*10*	*11*	*0*	*(1*
	6	5	4	3	2	1	0	11	10	9	8	7	(6
	G					H	J				I		(G
Sum 0:	*9*	*10*	*11*	*0*	*1*	*2*	*3*	*4*	*5*	*6*	*7*	*8*	*(9*
	3	2	1	0	11	10	9	8	7	6	5	4	(3

Since we know only one of the two cyclic intervals of the array, we cannot add a third sum scale to either pair of sum scales. The same chords may also be derived from paired difference scales:

Diff. 5:	5	4	3	2	1	0	11	10	9	8	7	6	(5
	0	11	10	9	8	7	6	5	4	3	2	1	(0
	A	C				D	F		B		E	G	(A
Diff. 6:	*4*	*5*	*6*	*7*	*8*	*9*	*10*	*11*	*0*	*1*	*2*	*3*	*(4*
	10	*11*	*0*	*1*	*2*	*3*	*4*	*5*	*6*	*7*	*8*	*9*	*(10*

Diff. 8:	*9*	*10*	*11*	*0*	*1*	*2*	*3*	*4*	*5*	*6*	*7*	*8*	*(9*
	1	*2*	*3*	*4*	*5*	*6*	*7*	*8*	*9*	*10*	*11*	*0*	*(1*
	G					H	J				I		(G
Diff. 9:	3	2	1	0	11	10	9	8	7	6	5	4	(3
	6	5	4	3	2	1	0	11	10	9	8	7	(6

Chord G may be interpreted as a link between the two segments of either table, since it contains both sum couples and both interval couples represented by the respective pairs of sum and difference scales.

If we now consider the connections between successive chords in the example, we find that their symmetrical relations may be consistently expressed in terms of two interval classes, 4 (or 8) and 5 (or 7), as can be seen in example 57. These relations may also be inferred from the differences in pitch-class numbers between the successive chords as they appear in the paired sum scales and paired difference scales given above. We have already determined that one of the set forms of the array has 4 or 8 as its cyclic interval, and it would seem reasonable to take 5 or 7 as the cyclic interval of the other set form. The latter would then be either p_4p_9 or its cognate, $i_{11}i_4$, or the respectively equivalent set forms of cyclic interval 7. A set form reduction of example 56 is given in example 58.

EXAMPLE 57

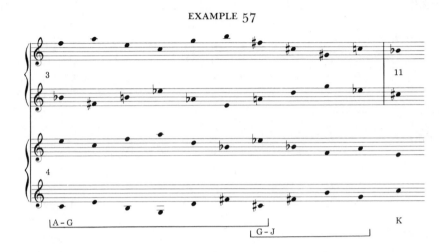

EXAMPLE 58

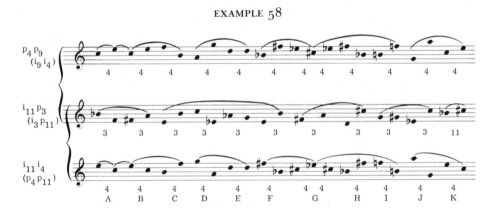

The paired sum scales above, comprising chords A through J, are shown in Table 35 in the context of the $p_4p_9/i_{11}p_3$ array. The brackets mark "tonic sum-tetrachords," so called by analogy with tonic cyclic chords. Two sum scales duplicating adjacency sums of the tonic set forms will always meet in the sum representation of an array, and where this happens interval 0, i.e., a duplicated pitch-class number, occurs as a component of the characteristic interval couple of the paired sum scales. Such a repetition, for example, occurs at the intersection of sum-scales 11 and 9 (see Table 35, below). Therefore the adjacency-sum 4, produced by the outer elements of each sum tetrachord of paired sum-scales 8 and 11, will also occur as a component of each cyclic chord in the series of tonic cyclic chords produced by the combined alternate sum scales 8 and 9. Similarly, the adjacency-sum 3, produced by the inner elements of each sum tetrachord of paired sum-scales 9 and 10, will also occur as a component of each cyclic chord in the series of tonic cyclic chords produced by the combined alternate sum scales 11 and 10.

Conversely, the tetrachords of sum-scales 8 and 11 will duplicate one of the cyclic intervals, 4, of sum-scales 8 and 9, and the tetrachords of sum-scales 9 and 10 will duplicate one of the cyclic intervals, 5, of sum-scales 11 and 10. **In general, cyclic chords represent only the cyclic intervals and sum tetrachords only the tonic sums of an array. Tonic cyclic chords are a special case in that they also represent sums, and tonic sum-tetrachords a special case in that they also represent cyclic intervals.** In addition, each bracketed tonic sum-tetrachord will duplicate, in one of its secondary sums, a tonic sum that is not represented in the adjacencies of the given tetrachord. Thus the sum tetrachords produced by paired sum-scales 4 and 4 each comprise a secondary sum that is equivalent to the tonic sum 4, and the sum tetrachords produced by paired sum-scales 3 and 5 each comprise a secondary sum that is equivalent to the tonic sum 3. The primary sum couple in each instance, however, is 11,9. Similarly, the sum tetrachords produced by paired sum-scales 8 and 11, and by paired sum-scales 9 and 10, have as a primary sum couple 4,3, and as one of their secondary sums either 11 or 9, equivalent to one or the other of the remaining tonic sums.

Each of the bracketed tonic sum-tetrachords will occur elsewhere in the sum table with the respective secondary and tertiary sums interchanged. The tonic sum-tetrachords generated by sum-scales 8 and 11, for example, recur with 8 and 11 as their tertiary sums, and with their earlier tertiary sums now represented as secondary sums. In this alternative representation each tonic sum-tetrachord overlaps with a second tonic sum-tetrachord to form an axis-dyad chord whose cyclic intervals share a common pitch-class number (Table 36). Because of this duplication, the primary intervals of the cyclic chord are repeated in the respective intervals of the neighbor-note dyads. Thus, for example, in the first axis-dyad chord in Table 36, dyads of pitch-classes 0,4 and 4,11 may be understood as either cyclic intervals or as neighbor-note dyads.

The semi-equivalent array, p_4p_9/i_3p_{11}, incorporates, in its difference table (Table 37), the two pairs of difference scales that serve as an alternative source of chords A through J of example 56. Brackets enclose the same series of tonic sum-tetrachords as in the preceding sum table of the $p_4p_9/i_{11}p_3$ array, but they now appear in the context of the axis-dyad chords shown in Table 36.

TABLE 35

Sum 3:	*10*	*11*	*0*	*1*	*2*	*3*	*4*	*5*	*6*	*7*	*8*	*9*	*(10*
	5	4	3	2	1	0	11	10	9	8	7	6	(5
Sum 4:	*10*	*11*	*0*	*1*	*2*	*3*	*4*	*5*	*6*	*7*	*8*	*9*	*(10*
	6	5	4	3	2	1	0	11	10	9	8	7	(6
Sum 4:	*3*	*4*	*5*	*6*	*7*	*8*	*9*	*10*	*11*	*0*	*1*	*2*	*(3*
	1	0	11	10	9	8	7	6	5	4	3	2	(1
Sum 3:	*2*	*3*	*4*	*5*	*6*	*7*	*8*	*9*	*10*	*11*	*0*	*1*	*(2*
	1	0	11	10	9	8	7	6	5	4	3	2	(1
Sum 5:	*8*	*9*	*10*	*11*	*0*	*1*	*2*	*3*	*4*	*5*	*6*	*7*	*(8*
	9	8	7	6	5	4	3	2	1	0	11	10	(9
Sum 2:	*6*	*7*	*8*	*9*	*10*	*11*	*0*	*1*	*2*	*3*	*4*	*5*	*(6*
	8	7	6	5	4	3	2	1	0	11	10	9	(8
Sum 6:	*1*	*2*	*3*	*4*	*5*	*6*	*7*	*8*	*9*	*10*	*11*	*0*	*(1*
	5	4	3	2	1	0	11	10	9	8	7	6	(5
Sum 1:	*10*	*11*	*0*	*1*	*2*	*3*	*4*	*5*	*6*	*7*	*8*	*9*	*(10*
	3	2	1	0	11	10	9	8	7	6	5	4	(3
Sum 7:	*6*	*7*	*8*	*9*	*10*	*11*	*0*	*1*	*2*	*3*	*4*	*5*	*(6*
	1	0	11	10	9	8	7	6	5	4	3	2	(1
Sum 0:	*2*	*3*	*4*	*5*	*6*	*7*	*8*	*9*	*10*	*11*	*0*	*1*	*(2*
	10	9	8	7	6	5	4	3	2	1	0	11	(10
Sum 8:	*11*	*0*	*1*	*2*	*3*	*4*	*5*	*6*	*7*	*8*	*9*	*10*	*(11*
	9	8	7	6	5	4	3	2	1	0	11	10	(9
Sum 11:	*6*	*7*	*8*	*9*	*10*	*11*	*0*	*1*	*2*	*3*	*4*	*5*	*(6*
	5	4	3	2	1	0	11	10	9	8	7	6	(5
Sum 9:	*4*	*5*	*6*	*7*	*8*	*9*	*10*	*11*	*0*	*1*	*2*	*3*	*(4*
	5	4	3	2	1	0	11	10	9	8	7	6	(5
Sum 10:	*10*	*11*	*0*	*1*	*2*	*3*	*4*	*5*	*6*	*7*	*8*	*9*	*(10*
	0	11	10	9	8	7	6	5	4	3	2	1	(0
Sum 10:	*9*	*10*	*11*	*0*	*1*	*2*	*3*	*4*	*5*	*6*	*7*	*8*	*(9*
	1	0	11	10	9	8	7	6	5	4	3	2	(1
Sum 9:	*2*	*3*	*4*	*5*	*6*	*7*	*8*	*9*	*10*	*11*	*0*	*1*	*(2*
	7	6	5	4	3	2	1	0	11	10	9	8	(7

TABLE 36

Sum 4:	*0*						*6*							
	4						10							
Sum 4:	*5*	*6*					*11*	*0*						
	11	10					5	4						
Sum 3:	*4*	*5*					*10*	*11*						
	11	10					5	4						
Sum 5:		*11*	*0*					*5*	*6*					
		6	5					0	11					
Sum 2:		*9*	*10*	*11*				*3*	*4*	*5*				
		5	4	3				11	10	9				
Sum 6:			*5*	*6*	*7*				*11*	*0*	*1*			
			1	0	11				7	6	5			
Sum 1:					*3*	*4*				*9*	*10*			
					10	9				4	3			
Sum 7:					*0*	*1*					*6*	*7*		
					7	6					1	0		
Sum 0:						*8*	*9*	*10*			*2*	*3*	*4*	
						4	3	2			10	9	8	
Sum 8:						*6*	*7*	*8*				*0*	*1*	*2*
						2	1	0				8	7	6
Sum 11:							*2*	*3*				*8*	*9*	
							9	8				3	2	
Sum 9:								*1*	*2*				*7*	*8*
								8	7				2	1
Sum 10:								*7*	*8*				*1*	*2*
								3	2				9	8
Sum 10:								*7*						*1*
								3						6

TABLE 37

Diff. 8:	5	6	7	8	9	10	11	0	1	2	3	4	(5
	9	10	11	0	1	2	3	4	5	6	7	8	(9
Diff. 9:	7	6	5	4	3	2	1	0	11	10	9	8	(7
	10	9	8	7	6	5	4	3	2	1	0	11	(10
Diff. 11:	1	2	3	4	5	6	7	8	9	10	11	0	(1
	2	3	4	5	6	7	8	9	10	11	0	1	(2
Diff. 0:	2	1	0	11	10	9	8	7	6	5	4	3	(2
	2	1	0	11	10	9	8	7	6	5	4	3	(2
Diff. 2:	9	10	11	0	1	2	3	4	5	6	7	8	(9
	7	8	9	10	11	0	1	2	3	4	5	6	(7
Diff. 3:	9	8	7	6	5	4	3	2	1	0	11	10	(9
	6	5	4	3	2	1	0	11	10	9	8	7	(6
Diff. 5:	5	6	7	8	9	10	11	0	1	2	3	4	(5
	0	1	2	3	4	5	6	7	8	9	10	11	(0
Diff. 6	4	3	2	1	0	11	10	9	8	7	6	5	(4
	10	9	8	7	6	5	4	3	2	1	0	11	(10
Diff. 8:	1	2	3	4	5	6	7	8	9	10	11	0	(1
	5	6	7	8	9	10	11	0	1	2	3	4	(5
Diff. 9:	11	10	9	8	7	6	5	4	3	2	1	0	(11
	2	1	0	11	10	9	8	7	6	5	4	3	(2
Diff. 10:	4	5	6	7	8	9	10	11	0	1	2	3	(4
	6	7	8	9	10	11	0	1	2	3	4	5	(6
Diff. 11:	10	9	8	7	6	5	4	3	2	1	0	11	(10
	11	10	9	8	7	6	5	4	3	2	1	0	(11
Diff. 1:	0	1	2	3	4	5	6	7	8	9	10	11	(0
	11	0	1	2	3	4	5	6	7	8	9	10	(11
Diff. 2:	5	4	3	2	1	0	11	10	9	8	7	6	(5
	3	2	1	0	11	10	9	8	7	6	5	4	(3
Diff. 4:	8	9	10	11	0	1	2	3	4	5	6	7	(8
	4	5	6	7	8	9	10	11	0	1	2	3	(4
Diff. 5:	0	11	10	9	8	7	6	5	4	3	2	1	(0
	7	6	5	4	3	2	1	0	11	10	9	8	(7
Diff. 7:	4	5	6	7	8	9	10	11	0	1	2	3	(4
	9	10	11	0	1	2	3	4	5	6	7	8	(9
Diff. 8:	7	6	5	4	3	2	1	0	11	10	9	8	(7
	11	10	9	8	7	6	5	4	3	2	1	0	(11

Left-hand brackets:
- Sums 9,10 — grouping Diff. 5 and Diff. 6
- Sums 3,5 — grouping Diff. 6 and Diff. 8
- Sums 8,11 — grouping Diff. 4 and Diff. 5
- Sums 4,4 — grouping Diff. 5 and Diff. 7
- Sums 8,11 — grouping Diff. 7 and Diff. 8

The sum version of $p_4p_9/i_{11}p_3$ and the difference version of the semi-equivalent array, p_4p_9/i_3p_{11}, contain different distributions of exactly the same collection of sum tetrachords and axis-dyad chords. Each column of the sum representation of the former array is duplicated, with each vertical dyad reversed, in a column of the *complete* difference representation of the latter array.[29] The first four columns in the sum table (p. 112), for example, are respectively represented as follows in the difference table (Table 38).

TABLE 38

Diff. 7:	5 10	Diff. 5:	4 11	Diff. 3:	3 0	Diff. 1:	2 1
Diff. 8:	6 10	Diff. 6:	5 11	Diff. 4:	4 0	Diff. 2:	3 1
Diff. 10:	1 3	Diff. 8:	0 4	Diff. 6:	11 5	Diff. 4:	10 6
Diff. 11:	1 2	Diff. 9:	0 3	Diff. 7:	11 4	Diff. 5:	10 5
Diff. 1:	9 8	Diff. 11:	8 9	Diff. 9:	7 10	Diff. 7:	6 11
etc.		etc.		etc.		etc.	

Sum tetrachords, like cyclic chords, may be interpreted as segments of derived sets. A derived set that unfolds a series of cyclic chords is generated by cycles that alternate the two cyclic intervals of the array. For the preceding $p_4p_9/i_{11}p_3$ sum array these intervals are 5 and 4. The tonic derived set form $p_4(5,4)$, for example, unfolds the cyclic chords of sum-scales 8 and 9 as follows:

```
 3  5 ⌐11  10⌐6   2⌐2   7⌐9  11⌐5   4⌐0   8⌐8   1 ⌐(3   5⌐  ‖
 4)  4⌐0   9⌐7   1⌐3   6⌐10  (10⌐6   3⌐1   7⌐9   0⌐4   4⌐
```

The tonic derived set form $p_9(5,4)$ unfolds the cyclic chords of sum-scales 4 and 5:

29. Cf. p. 89, above. The last two scales in the second partition of Table 37, 7 and 8, are respectively equivalent to the scales of the complementary interval numbers, 5 and 4. A continuation would similarly repeat the preceding scales, substituting the complementary number for each. A complete representation would also entail a third partition, in which the succession of difference scales in the first partition would be reversed and the complementary difference number substituted for each scale. (Cf. the twelfth column of the first partition above with the third column of Table 38.)

⌊3 1 ⌈8 9⌋⌊0 4⌋5 0⌊⌊9 7⌋⌊2 3⌋⌊6 10⌋⌊11 6⌋(3 1⌉ ‖

⌊2) 2 ⌈7 10⌋⌊11 5⌋⌊4 1⌋⌊8 (8⌊⌊1 4⌋⌊5 11⌋⌊10 7⌋2 2⌋

The remaining tonic derived set forms, $i_{11}(4,5)$ and $p_3(4,5)$, similarly unfold the cyclic chords of sum-scales 3,4 and 11,10 respectively. Cyclic chords formed by other pairs of sum scales will occur as segments of resultant set forms, that is, other members of the same set complex, generated by cycles that likewise alternate intervals 4 and 5. For example, p_{11}, a T(1) transposition of $p_9(5,4)$, unfolds the cyclic chords of sum-scales 6 and 7:

⌊4 2 ⌈9 10⌋⌊1 5⌋⌊6 1⌋ . . ⌉ .

A T(11) transposition, p_2, of $p_4(5,4)$ produces an alternative version of the same series of cyclic chords:

⌊2 4 ⌈10 9⌋⌊5 1⌋⌊1 6⌋ . . ⌉ .

Every derived set form that unfolds a series of sum tetrachords, on the other hand, is based on a tonic adjacency sum. However, the cyclic interval associated with that sum in the set forms that generate the array, p_4p_9 and $i_{11}p_3$, is preserved only for the derived set forms that unfold the tonic sum-tetrachords. These tonic set forms are $p_4(5,6)$ (we will show the cyclic interval on the left in naming the derived set) for the tetrachords produced by pairing sum-scales 9 and 10,

⌊4 5 ⌈11) 11⌋⌊5 4⌈0 10⌋6 3⌈1 9⌋7 2⌈2 8⌋8 1⌈3 7⌋9 0⌈4 6⌋⌊10 11⌈5 (5⌋11 10⌉

$p_9(5,5)$ for the tetrachords produced by pairing sum-scales 4 and 4,

⌊9 7 ⌈2) 2⌋⌊7 9⌈0 4⌋⌊5 11⌈10 6⌋⌊3 1⌈8 (8⌊1 3⌉

$i_{11}(4,6)$ for the tetrachords produced by pairing sum-scales 3 and 5,

⌊5 0 ⌈11 4⌋⌊7 10⌈1 2⌋⌊9 8⌈3 0⌋⌊11 6⌈5 10⌋⌊1 4⌈7 8⌋⌊3 2⌈9 6⌋⌊(5 0⌈11 4⌋

and $p_3(4,7)$ for the tetrachords produced by pairing sum-scales 8 and 11,

⌊0 11⌈4) 4⌋⌊11 0⌈3 5⌋⌊10 1⌈2 6⌋⌊9 2⌈1 7⌋⌊8 3⌈0 8⌋⌊7 4⌈11 9⌋⌊6 5⌈10 (10⌊5 6⌉

All the chords of example 56 except H, I, and K occur as segments of the tonic derived set form, $p_4(5,6)$:

```
                                      ┌── D,J ──┐┌── F ──┐
4 5 11) 11  5 4 0 10  6 3 1 9  7 2 2 8  8 1 3 7  9 0 4 6  10 11 5 (5 11 10
└── C ──┘└── A ──┘└── G ──┘└── E ──┘           └──── B ────┘
```

Each series of sum tetrachords may be expressed through either of two cognate-related derived set forms, as shown in Table 39.[30] Tonic derived set forms are given in italics.

---

30. "Cognate-related" derived set forms are not necessarily inversionally related, but, like inversionally-related basic set forms that share a tonic sum (cf. p. 20, above), they may

TABLE 39

Sums $\frac{4}{4}$ $p_9(5,5)$ $i_{11}(5,5)$

                     Sums $\frac{4}{3}$ $p_4(0,11)$ $p_3(0,11)$

Sums $\frac{3}{5}$ $p_9(4,6)$ $i_{11}(4,6)$

                     Sums $\frac{5}{2}$ $p_4(1,10)$ $p_3(1,10)$

Sums $\frac{2}{6}$ $p_9(3,7)$ $i_{11}(3,7)$

                     Sums $\frac{6}{1}$ $p_4(2,9)$ $p_3(2,9)$

Sums $\frac{1}{7}$ $p_9(2,8)$ $i_{11}(2,8)$

                     Sums $\frac{7}{0}$ $p_4(3,8)$ $p_3(3,8)$

Sums $\frac{0}{8}$ $p_9(1,9)$ $i_{11}(1,9)$

                     Sums $\frac{8}{11}$ $p_4(4,7)$ $p_3(4,7)$

Sums $\frac{11}{9}$ $p_9(0,10)$ $i_{11}(0,10)$

                     Sums $\frac{9}{10}$ $p_4(5,6)$ $p_3(5,6)$

Sums $\frac{10}{10}$ $p_9(11,11)$ $i_{11}(11,11)$

The same sum tetrachords in the semi-equivalent array, p_4p_9/i_3p_{11}, unfold as segments of the same derived set forms, but i_{11} and p_3 are respectively renamed p_{11} and i_3 and their cyclic interval numbers replaced by the complementary interval numbers. For example, tetrachords of secondary sum-couple 1,7 as represented in Table 37 are formed by paired difference-scales 2 and 4 and occur as segments of $p_9(2,8)$ or $p_{11}(10,4)$. (The cyclic intervals of the derived set forms may be inferred from the difference numbers of the paired scales. One of the two cyclic interval numbers of each set form coincides with one of the difference numbers assigned to the paired scales; the other of the two cyclic interval numbers coincides with the complement of the other of the two difference numbers.) In the sum array each series of tonic sum-tetrachords unfolds in two adjacent scales, the sum number of one of which will

———————

be segmented into series of dyads that are identical except for the order of pitch-class components of each dyad.

coincide with a tonic sum number. We derive the first chord of example 56, for instance, from the following sum alignment of the basic set forms of the array, which we can read from the first column in Table 35:

p₄p₉:	*10*	6	*3*	1	*8*	8	*1*	3	6	10	*11*	5	4	0	*9*	*7*
p₃i₁₁:	5	*10*	1	2	9	6	5	*10*	1	2	9	6	5	*10*	1	2
Sums:	3̄	4̄	4̄	3̄	5̄	2̄	6̄	1̄	7̄	0̄	8̄	11̄	9̄	10̄	10̄	9̄

This tonic sum-tetrachord may be expanded into an axis-dyad chord by the addition of a neighbor-note dyad of sum 11, one of whose elements, pitch-class 5, is already contained in the sum tetrachord. Tonic-sum 9, already represented in the sum tetrachord, is now represented as an adjacency as well, and tonic-sum 11 is similarly represented in the completed axis-dyad chord as both an adjacency and a vertical dyad. The same tonic sum-tetrachord is found in the following difference alignment of the basic set forms of the semi-equivalent array, which we can read from the first column in Table 37:

p₄p₉:	*9*	7	*2*	2	7	*9*	0	4	5	11
i₃p₁₁:	5	10	*1*	2	9	6	5	*10*	*1*	2
Intervals:	8	9	11	0	2	3	5	6	8	9

The tonic sum-tetrachord may here be expanded into an axis-dyad chord by the addition of a neighbor-note dyad of difference 8. As before, an element of the latter, pitch-class 5, is already contained in the sum tetrachord. The elements of cyclic-interval 5 (pitch-classes 0 and 5), already present in the sum tetrachord, are now cyclically unfolded as well, and interval 8 is similarly represented in the axis-dyad chord as both a cyclic interval and a vertical dyad.

As noted above, **a tonic sum-tetrachord, like a tonic cyclic chord, is a segment of a tonic derived set form, and its neighboring dyad, like the axis-note dyad of the tonic cyclic chord, is equivalent to a defining element—either a tonic sum, or a cyclic interval—of the associated set form.** For example:[31]

p₄(5,6):	(	5	4	0	(10)
p₃(4,7):		6	5	10	
Sums:		11	9	10	

p₄(5,6):	(10)	0	4	5	)
p₃(4,7):			5	10	1
Sums:			5	2	6
(Intervals:			5		4)

31. In the second p₄(5,6)/p₃(4,7) chord we show the intervals, in parentheses below the diagram, of the axis-dyad chord produced by the *sum alignment*. When the two neighbor-note dyads are read in opposite directions their interval numbers are equivalent to the cyclic interval numbers.

or, in the semi-equivalent array,

$p_4(5,6)$: (10) | 0   4 | 5)
$i_3(8,5)$: | 5   10 | 1 /

Intervals: 5   6   8

$p_4(5,6)$: (10) | 0   4 | 5)
$i_3(8,5)$: | 10   5 | 6 /

Intervals: 10   11   1

(Sums: 9   11)

Axis-dyad chords formed by the combination of a tonic sum-tetrachord and a neighboring tonic sum are the same as those formed by the combination of a tonic cyclic chord and a tonic axis-note dyad:

$$p_4(5,4)$$:   5   4   0
$$p_3(4,5)$$:   6   5   10   (0)

Sums: 11   9   10

or, in the semi-equivalent array,

$$p_{11}(8,5)$$:   10   5   6   (0)
$$p_9(5,8)$$:   0   4   5

Intervals: 10   11   1

(Sums: 9   11)

Axis-dyad chords of this type are characterized by the duplication of a primary sum couple in the relations between vertically associated pitch classes of the aligned set segments. We shall call such chords "sum-type axis-dyad chords." Where, instead, the primary intervals of a cyclic chord are duplicated, the axis-note dyad may be combined with either of its neighboring dyads to form a tonic sum-tetrachord:

$p_4(5,6)$: (10) | 0   4 | 5
$p_3(4,7)$: | 5   10 | 1

Sums: 5   2   6

(Intervals: 5   4)

$p_9(5,5)$:   0 | 4   5 |
$i_{11}(4,6)$:   5 | 10   1 | (4)

Sums: 5   2   6

(Intervals: 5   4)

or, in the semi-equivalent array,

$p_4(5,6)$: (10) | 0   4 | 5
$i_3(8,5)$: | 5   10 | 1

Intervals: 5   6   8

$p_9(5,5)$:   0 | 4   5 |
$p_{11}(8,6)$:   5 | 10   1 | (4)

Intervals: 5   6   8

Axis-dyad chords of this type, consisting of overlapping tonic sum-tetrachords, will be termed "interval-type axis-dyad chords."

The table of difference scales of $p_4p_9/i_{11}p_3$ (Table 40) duplicates the axis-dyad chords of the sum-scale table (Table 35), but not its sum tetrachords, since the difference array (i.e., the mode) aligns sum 4 with sum 11 and sum 9 with sum 3, while the sum array (i.e., the key) aligns sum 4 with sum 3 and sum 9 with sum 11. Correspondences between the difference array of $p_4p_9/i_{11}p_3$ and the sum array of p_4p_9/i_3p_{11} will be exactly analogous to those, noted above, between the difference array of the latter and the sum array of the former.

The brackets mark overlapping tonic sum-tetrachords that generate interval-type axis-dyad chords. The axis-dyad sum of each of these chords shows where the same chord can be found in the sum array. Since the sum array pairs cyclic intervals of opposite aspect, where the difference array pairs cyclic intervals of the same aspect, the neighbor-note dyads are not the same. The characteristic interval-type axis-dyad chords of the sum array (cf. p. 113, above), are correspondingly reordered in the difference array. In the cyclic intervals of each such chord there is a repeated pitch class, and these become the dyads of difference scale 0 in the difference array. The interval-type axis-dyad chords of the sum array are thus duplicated in difference-scales 1, 7, 0 and difference-scales 0, 6, 11. The complete collection of tonic sum-tetrachords of the difference array is comprised in the following tonic derived set forms:

$p_4(5,2)$: ⌊8 *1* ⌐3) 3⌋₁1 8⌐⌐8 10⌋₁6 3⌐ ⌐1 5⌋₁11 10⌐ 6 0₁₁4 5⌐⌐11 7⌋₁9 0⌐ 4 2₁₁2 7⌐⌐9 (9₁ 7

$i_{11}(4,1)$: ⌊4 *11*⌐0) 0⌋₁11 4⌐⌐7 5⌋₁6 9⌐⌐2 10⌋₁1 2⌐⌐9 3⌋₁8 7⌐⌐4 8⌋₁3 0⌐⌐11 1⌋₁10 5⌐⌐6 (6₁ 5

$p_9(5,1)$: ⌊*1* 7⌐*2*) 2⌋₁*7 1*⌐⌐*8* (8₁ *1 7*⌐ ⌐⌐⌐0 8⌐*1 3*₁6 2⌐*7 9*₁(0 8⌐
  ⌊*5 11*⌐*10*) *10*⌋₁*11 5*⌐*4* (4₁*5 11*⌐ ⌐⌐⌐4 0⌐*9* 11₁₁*10 6*⌐*3 7*₁(4 0⌐

$p_3(4,2)$: ⌊*11 0*⌐*3 10*₁5 6⌐*9 4*₁(11 0⌐ ⌐⌐⌐10 1⌐*2 11*₁₁4 7⌐*8 5*₁(10 1⌐
  ⌊*9 2*⌐*1 0*₁*3 8*⌐*7 6*₁(*9 2*⌐

All sum tetrachords of the difference array occur as segments of derived set forms as indicated in Table 41.

TABLE 40

Diff. 10:	2	3	4	5	6	7	8	9	10	11	0	1	(2
	4	5	6	7	8	9	10	11	0	1	2	3	(4
Diff. 3:	0	11	10	9	8	7	6	5	4	3	2	1	(0
	9	8	7	6	5	4	3	2	1	0	11	10	(9
Diff. 9:	6	7	8	9	10	11	0	1	2	3	4	5	(6
	9	10	11	0	1	2	3	4	5	6	7	8	(9
Diff. 2:	7	6	5	4	3	2	1	0	11	10	9	8	(7
	5	4	3	2	1	0	11	10	9	8	7	6	(5
Diff. 8:	10	11	0	1	2	3	4	5	6	7	8	9	(10
	2	3	4	5	6	7	8	9	10	11	0	1	(2
Diff. 1:	2	1	0	11	10	9	8	7	6	5	4	3	(2
	1	0	11	10	9	8	7	6	5	4	3	2	(1
Diff. 7:	2	3	4	5	6	7	8	9	10	11	0	1	(2
	7	8	9	10	11	0	1	2	3	4	5	6	(7
Diff. 0:	9	8	7	6	5	4	3	2	1	0	11	10	(9
	9	8	7	6	5	4	3	2	1	0	11	10	(9
Diff. 6:	6	7	8	9	10	11	0	1	2	3	4	5	(6
	0	1	2	3	4	5	6	7	8	9	10	11	(0
Diff. 11:	4	3	2	1	0	11	10	9	8	7	6	5	(4
	5	4	3	2	1	0	11	10	9	8	7	6	(5
Diff. 5:	10	11	0	1	2	3	4	5	6	7	8	9	(10
	5	6	7	8	9	10	11	0	1	2	3	4	(5
Diff. 10:	11	10	9	8	7	6	5	4	3	2	1	0	(11
	1	0	11	10	9	8	7	6	5	4	3	2	(1
Diff. 4:	2	3	4	5	6	7	8	9	10	11	0	1	(2
	10	11	0	1	2	3	4	5	6	7	8	9	(10
Diff. 9:	6	5	4	3	2	1	0	11	10	9	8	7	(6
	9	8	7	6	5	4	3	2	1	0	11	10	(9
Diff. 3:	6	7	8	9	10	11	0	1	2	3	4	5	(6
	3	4	5	6	7	8	9	10	11	0	1	2	(3
Diff. 8:	1	0	11	10	9	8	7	6	5	4	3	2	(1
	5	4	3	2	1	0	11	10	9	8	7	6	(5

TABLE 41

Diff. $\begin{smallmatrix}3\\9\end{smallmatrix}$ $p_9(3,3)$ $p_3(9,9)$

Diff. $\begin{smallmatrix}9\\2\end{smallmatrix}$ $i_{11}(3,2)$ $p_4(9,10)$

Diff. $\begin{smallmatrix}2\\8\end{smallmatrix}$ $p_9(4,2)$ $p_3(8,10)$

Diff. $\begin{smallmatrix}8\\1\end{smallmatrix}$ *$i_{11}(4,1)$* $p_4(8,11)$

Diff. $\begin{smallmatrix}1\\7\end{smallmatrix}$ *$p_9(5,1)$* $p_3(7,11)$

Diff. $\begin{smallmatrix}7\\0\end{smallmatrix}$ $i_{11}(5,0)$ $p_4(7,0)$

Diff. $\begin{smallmatrix}0\\6\end{smallmatrix}$ $p_9(6,0)$ $p_3(6,0)$

Diff. $\begin{smallmatrix}6\\11\end{smallmatrix}$ $i_{11}(6,11)$ $p_4(6,1)$

Diff. $\begin{smallmatrix}11\\5\end{smallmatrix}$ $p_9(7,11)$ $p_3(5,1)$

Diff. $\begin{smallmatrix}5\\10\end{smallmatrix}$ $i_{11}(7,10)$ *$p_4(5,2)$*

Diff. $\begin{smallmatrix}10\\4\end{smallmatrix}$ $p_9(8,10)$ *$p_3(4,2)$*

Diff. $\begin{smallmatrix}4\\9\end{smallmatrix}$ $i_{11}(8,9)$ $p_4(4,3)$

Diff. $\begin{smallmatrix}9\\3\end{smallmatrix}$ $p_9(9,9)$ $p_3(3,3)$

25. Modulation Through Tonic Cyclic Chords and Tonic Sum-Tetrachords

We have shown earlier (pp. 35f., 56ff.) how a tonic cyclic chord may serve as a pivotal connection between arrays of the same interval system and modal class,[32] but of different keys. Let us again consider the sum table of $p_4p_9/i_{11}p_3$ (Table 35). The neighbor-note dyads of any tonic axis-dyad sum will, as we have seen, give us tonic cyclic chords. Take, for example, the alignment of sum scales 8, 11, and 9 (Table 42).

TABLE 42

Sum 8:	*11*	*0*	*1*	*2*	*3*	*4*	*5*	*6*	*7*	*8*	*9*	*10*	*(11*
	9	8	7	6	5	4	3	2	1	0	11	10	(9
Sum 11:	*6*	*7*	*8*	*9*	*10*	*11*	*0*	*1*	*2*	*3*	*4*	*5*	*(6*
	5	4	3	2	1	0	11	10	9	8	7	6	(5
Sum 9:	*4*	*5*	*6*	*7*	*8*	*9*	*10*	*11*	*0*	*1*	*2*	*3*	*(4*
	5	4	3	2	1	0	11	10	9	8	7	6	(5

Since 11 is a tonic sum, its neighbor-note dyads form tonic cyclic chords. This property derives, as explained above (pp. 110f.), from the fact that a series of pitch-class numbers in the sum-9 scale is duplicated at interval 0 in the sum-11 scale. If each axis dyad of sum 11 is replaced by another of the same interval but a different sum which likewise results in the duplication of a series of pitch-class numbers, sum-scales 8 and 9 will generate the same series of tonic cyclic chords in relation to a new series of tonic axis dyads. Three new arrays, each of which will duplicate at least one of the original tonic sums, will be formed by this means. They are p_8p_1/i_3p_7, a T(2) or T(8) transposition of the original array, generated by the addition of 4 to each of the original sums (Table 43); p_2p_7/i_9p_1, a T(5) or T(11) transposition of the original array, generated by the addition of 10 to each of the original sums (Table 44); and i_9i_2/p_4i_8, generated by the addition of 5 to each of the original sums, but not transpositionally equivalent to the original array, since 5 is odd (Table 45). The transpositions of the original axis-dyad sum scale, T(0), T(4), T(10), T(5), by which these modulations are affected correspond to the interval system ($10-5=5$, $4-0=4$) and mode ($5-0=5$, $10-4=6$) shared by the four arrays.

32. Cf. n. 25, p. 88.

TABLE 43

Sum 8:	11	0	1	2	3	4	5	6	7	8	9	10	(11
	9	8	7	6	5	4	3	2	1	0	11	10	(9

Sum 7:	10	11	0	1	2	3	4	5	6	7	8	9	(10
	9	8	7	6	5	4	3	2	1	0	11	10	(9

Sum 9:	4	5	6	7	8	9	10	11	0	1	2	3	(4
	5	4	3	2	1	0	11	10	9	8	7	6	(5

TABLE 44

Sum 8:	11	0	1	2	3	4	5	6	7	8	9	10	(11
	9	8	7	6	5	4	3	2	1	0	11	10	(9

Sum 7:	4	5	6	7	8	9	10	11	0	1	2	3	(4
	3	2	1	0	11	10	9	8	7	6	5	4	(3

Sum 9:	4	5	6	7	8	9	10	11	0	1	2	3	(4
	5	4	3	2	1	0	11	10	9	8	7	6	(5

TABLE 45

Sum 8:	11	0	1	2	3	4	5	6	7	8	9	10	(11
	9	8	7	6	5	4	3	2	1	0	11	10	(9

Sum 9:	11	0	1	2	3	4	5	6	7	8	9	10	(11
	10	9	8	7	6	5	4	3	2	1	0	11	(10

Sum 9:	4	5	6	7	8	9	10	11	0	1	2	3	(4
	5	4	3	2	1	0	11	10	9	8	7	6	(5

The analogous operations relative to the tonic cyclic chords given by sum-scales 11 and 10 in the original array will result in a T(7) transposition of the original axis-dyad scale to produce the $i_{11}i_4/p_6i_{10}$ array, a T(2) transposition of the original axis-dyad scale to produce the p_6p_{11}/i_1p_5 array, and a T(6) transposition of the original axis-dyad scale to produce the $p_{10}p_3/i_5p_9$ array. The original alignment of sum-scales 4, 4, and 3 may be similarly converted, through T(5), T(7), and T(11) transpositions of the axis-dyad scale, to produce, respectively, i_9i_2/p_4i_8, $i_{11}i_4/p_6i_{10}$, and $i_3i_8/p_{10}i_2$; and the original alignment of sum-scales 4, 3, and 5 may be similarly converted, through T(8), T(6), and T(1) transpositions of the axis-dyad scale, to produce, respectively, p_0p_5/i_7p_{11}, $p_{10}p_3/i_5p_9$, and i_5i_{10}/p_0i_4.

All the arrays of cyclic-intervals 5 and 4 in Mode 5,6 are shown in Table 46.[33] Of these arrays, those, and only those, that share a tonic sum

33. Each array in Table 46 is found by adding a constant integer to each sum of the original array. **The addition of the same even number to each sum in the name of an array preserves the same aspect names for corresponding sums and results in a transposition of the array. The addition of the same odd number to each sum in the name of**

TABLE 46

C1	C2	C3	C4	Name
4	11	8	4	
4	9	11	3	$p_4p_9/i_{11}p_3$
3	10	9	5	

C1	C2	C3	C4	Name
			4	
			5	i_5i_{10}/p_0i_4
			5	
	11			
	1			p_6p_{11}/i_1p_5
	10			
				i_7i_0/p_2i_6
		8		
		7		p_8p_1/i_3p_7
		9		
4		8		
2		9		i_9i_2/p_4i_8
3		9		
	11		4	
	9		3	$p_{10}p_3/i_5p_9$
	10		5	
4	11			
6	11			$i_{11}i_4/p_6i_{10}$
3	10			
			4	
			7	p_0p_5/i_7p_{11}
			5	
				i_1i_6/p_8i_0
		8		
		7		p_2p_7/i_9p_1
		9		
4				
2				$i_3i_8/p_{10}i_2$
3				

an array results in the substitution of the opposite aspect name for corresponding sums. The two arrays will be in the same modal class but they will not be transposable or invertible into one another. The subtraction of each sum in the name of an array from the same even number results in the substitution of opposite aspect names and with the original array will intersect with that array through a series of tonic cyclic chords. The segments of the sum table that comprise these connections and the required substitutions of axis-dyad scales are indicated at the left.

In each case, the transpositions of a given tonic axis-dyad scale correspond to the cyclic intervals and mode of the array, and therefore duplicate the structure of the cyclic chords of axis-interval 0. In example 59 the various transpositions of the bass line relative to the fixed upper voices reflect this property.

EXAMPLE 59

Perle, Serenade No. 1, IV (1962)

Copyright 1975 by Columbia University press.
Galaxy Music Corporation, sole agent.
Used by permission.

produces an inversionally related array. Thus, for example, $p_4p_9/i_{11}p_3$ is inverted into i_8i_3/p_1i_9 by the subtraction of each of its sums from 0. Table 46 does not include the arrays found by subtraction from a constant sum. These would be in the complementary mode, 7,6. (Cf. n. 25.)

Since the cyclic chords in example 59 are consistently based on axis dyads of a single interval number, it is convenient to refer them to the difference tables of the respective arrays. The common tonic cyclic chord exploited in the example as a means of modulation is shown in the initial column of the given difference-scale alignment. The four arrays that share this chord are $p_{10}p_5/i_1i_8$ (Table 47); p_4p_{11}/i_1i_8, found by shifting the setting of the axis-interval scale in Table 47 three places to the left; p_8p_3/i_5i_0, found by shifting the axis-interval scale four additional places to the left; and $p_8p_3/i_{11}i_6$, found by shifting the latter setting of the axis-interval scale three additional places to the left. Thus the pitch classes of the pivotal cyclic chord and those of the successive tonic axis dyads are the same, 5, 8, 0, and 3.

TABLE 47

Diff. 9:	0	11	10	9	8	7	6	5	4	3	2	1	(0
	3	2	1	0	11	10	9	8	7	6	5	4	(3
Diff. 0:	5	6	7	8	9	10	11	0	1	2	3	4	(5
	5	6	7	8	9	10	11	0	1	2	3	4	(5
Diff. 9:	5	4	3	2	1	0	11	10	9	8	7	6	(5
	8	7	6	5	4	3	2	1	0	11	10	9	(8

Modulation through a pivotal tonic cyclic chord may also be effected by replacing the original tonic axis dyad by another of the same sum but different interval, rather than by another of the same interval but different sum. As before, the shift must in each case result in the duplication of a series of pitch-class numbers. Where formerly the mode (or modal class) and interval system were retained and the key was changed, now the key and the interval system are retained and the mode is changed. Let us again refer to the alignment of sum-scales 8, 11, and 9 of the $p_4p_9/i_{11}p_3$ array (Table 35). A shift of the axis-dyad scale five places to the left converts the array to $i_{11}i_4/p_4i_8$. If the original setting of sum-scale 11 is shifted eight places to the left the original array is converted to p_8p_1/i_7p_{11}. A shift of ten places to the left converts the original array to p_6p_{11}/i_9p_1.

Analogous operations relative to the tonic cyclic chords given by sum-scales 11 and 10 in the $p_4p_9/i_{11}p_3$ array (Table 35) require a shift of two places in the original setting of sum-scale 9, to produce p_6p_{11}/i_9p_1, a shift of five places to produce i_9i_2/p_6i_{10}, and a shift of six places to produce $p_{10}p_3/i_5p_9$. The original alignment of sum-scales 4, 4, and 3 may be similarly converted, through shifts in the axis-dyad scale of seven places to produce $i_{11}i_4/p_4i_8$, and of eleven places to produce i_3i_8/p_0i_4. Finally, the original alignment of sum-scales 4, 3, and 5 may be similarly converted, through shifts in the axis-dyad scale of one place to produce i_3i_8/p_0i_4, four places to produce p_0p_5/i_3p_7, and of six places to produce $p_{10}p_3/i_5p_9$. In every case the key is the same, 7/8. Every representation of that key produced by pairing set forms of cyclic-intervals 5 and 4 respectively and duplicating one or more of the original tonic sums will share at least one series of tonic cyclic chords with the original array. All the arrays of cyclic-intervals 5 and 4 in the given key are shown in Table 48. The segments of the sum table that comprise the tonic-chord connections with the original array are indicated at the left.

TABLE 48

C1	C2	C3	C4	Label
4	11	8	4	
4	9	11	3	$P_4P_9/i_{11}P_3$
3	10	9	5	

C1	C2	C3	C4	Label
				$i_5i_{10}/P_{10}i_2$
	11	8		
	9	11		P_6P_{11}/i_9P_1
	10	9		
				i_7i_0/P_8i_0
		8		
		11		P_8P_1/i_7P_{11}
		9		
	11			
	9			i_9i_2/P_6i_{10}
	10			
	11		4	
	9		3	$P_{10}P_3/i_5P_9$
	10		5	
4		8		
4		11		$i_{11}i_4/P_4i_8$
3		9		
			4	
			3	P_0P_5/i_3P_7
			5	
				i_1i_6/P_2i_6
				P_2P_7/i_1P_5
4			4	
4			3	i_3i_8/P_2i_4
3			5	

Tonic sum-tetrachords are analogous to tonic cyclic chords in providing connections between different arrays. Where we previously effected the modulation from one array to another by a revision of either the sum or the interval of the axis notes of the cyclic chord, we now effect the modulation by a revision of either the sum or the interval of a neighbor-note dyad of the tonic sum-tetrachord. Let us again refer to the alignment of sum-scales 8, 11, and 9 of our original array, $p_4p_9/i_{11}p_3$ (Table 35). The tonic sum-tetrachords of primary sum-couple 4,3 given by the bracketed sum scales 8 and 11 are components of sum-type axis-dyad chords. The latter are completed by the series of neighbor-note dyads of a scale whose sum coincides with one of the tonic sums of the array, 9, and which doubles a series of pitch-class numbers of the adjacent scale of sum 11. A shift of sum-scale 9 two places to the left results in a duplication, instead, of the other series of pitch classes of sum-scale 11, and converts the original interval system (5,4) into another (7,6) in the same master array. The new array, p_4p_{11}/i_9p_3, is in Mode 7,8, where the original array was in Mode 5,6. The key, however, is the same (7,8) for both arrays. Equivalent shifts of sum-scale 11 in the opposite direction produce the same conversions of the original array relative to the tonic sum-tetrachords given by the bracketed sum scales 9 and 10. The reciprocal changes may be represented by shifting sum-scales 9 and 10 together two places to the left relative to sum-scales 8 and 11 (Table 49).

TABLE 49

Sum 8:	*11*	*0*	*1*	*2*	*3*	*4*	*5*	*6*	*7*	*8*	*9*	*10*	*(11*
	9	8	7	6	5	4	3	2	1	0	11	10	(9
Sum 11:	*6*	*7*	*8*	*9*	*10*	*11*	*0*	*1*	*2*	*3*	*4*	*5*	*(6*
	5	4	3	2	1	0	11	10	9	8	7	6	(5
Sum 9:	*6*	*7*	*8*	*9*	*10*	*11*	*0*	*1*	*2*	*3*	*4*	*5*	*(6*
	3	2	1	0	11	10	9	8	7	6	5	4	(3
Sum 10:	*0*	*1*	*2*	*3*	*4*	*5*	*6*	*7*	*8*	*9*	*10*	*11*	*(0*
	10	9	8	7	6	5	4	3	2	1	0	11	(10

The equivalent array, $i_3p_9/i_{11}i_4$, is derived when the analogous operation is applied to the other pair of bracketed sum scales, which mark the tonic sum-tetrachords of primary sum-couple 9,11. A shift of sum-scales 3 and 5 one place to the left relative to sum-scales 4 and 4 will provide the new unison doubling between adjacent sum scales (Table 50).

The modulatory implications of the tonic sum-tetrachords where these are components of interval-type axis-dyad chords (see p. 119, above) are easier to comprehend if we examine the latter in the context of the difference table of the semi-equivalent array, p_4p_9/i_3p_{11} (Table 37). Let us take the given setting of difference-scales 5, 6, and 8. We will assume that the tonic sum-tetrachords of primary-sums 11 and 9 (given by the bracketed difference scales, 6 and 8) are to be retained in the new array. A shift of difference-scale 5 one place to the left will give us a new series of shared pitch-class numbers between the cyclic intervals (Table 51).

TABLE 50

	10	*11*	*0*	*1*	*2*	*3*	*4*	*5*	*6*	*7*	*8*	*9*	*(10*
Sum 4:	6	5	4	3	2	1	0	11	10	9	8	7	(6

	3	*4*	*5*	*6*	*7*	*8*	*9*	*10*	*11*	*0*	*1*	*2*	*(3*
Sum 4:	1	0	11	10	9	8	7	6	5	4	3	2	(1

	3	*4*	*5*	*6*	*7*	*8*	*9*	*10*	*11*	*0*	*1*	*2*	*(3*
Sum 3:	0	11	10	9	8	7	6	5	4	3	2	1	(0

	9	*10*	*11*	*0*	*1*	*2*	*3*	*4*	*5*	*6*	*7*	*8*	*(9*
Sum 5:	8	7	6	5	4	3	2	1	0	11	10	9	(8

TABLE 51

Diff. 5:	*6*	*7*	*8*	*9*	*10*	*11*	*0*	*1*	*2*	*3*	*4*	*5*	*(6*
	1	*2*	*3*	*4*	*5*	*6*	*7*	*8*	*9*	*10*	*11*	*0*	*(1*

Diff. 6:	4	3	2	1	0	11	10	9	8	7	6	5	(4
	10	9	8	7	6	5	4	3	2	1	0	11	(10

Diff. 8:	*1*	*2*	*3*	*4*	*5*	*6*	*7*	*8*	*9*	*10*	*11*	*0*	*(1*
	5	*6*	*7*	*8*	*9*	*10*	*11*	*0*	*1*	*2*	*3*	*4*	*(5*

The original array of cyclic-intervals 5 and 8 is thus converted into an array of intervals 4 and 7: i_5p_9/p_4p_{11}. The mode, 1,10, is the same, but the key, 4,1, is new. The new interval system is the complement of the original interval system, and the two arrays are inversionally complementary to one another at sum 8:

$$\begin{Bmatrix} p_4p_9/i_3p_{11} \\ p_4p_{11}/i_5p_9 \end{Bmatrix} \quad \left(\text{is equivalent to} \begin{Bmatrix} p_4p_9/i_3p_{11} \\ i_4i_{11}/p_5i_9 \end{Bmatrix} \right)$$

If we assume that the tonic sum-tetrachords of primary-sums 4 and 3 (given by the bracketed difference scales, 5 and 6) are to be retained in the new array, we shift difference-scale 8 one place to the right to provide a new doubling of pitch-class numbers between the cyclic intervals (Table 52).

TABLE 52

Diff. 5:	*5*	*6*	*7*	*8*	*9*	*10*	*11*	*0*	*1*	*2*	*3*	*4*	*(5*
	0	*1*	*2*	*3*	*4*	*5*	*6*	*7*	*8*	*9*	*10*	*11*	*(0*
Diff. 6:	4	3	2	1	0	11	10	9	8	7	6	5	(4
	10	9	8	7	6	5	4	3	2	1	0	11	(10
Diff. 8:	*0*	*1*	*2*	*3*	*4*	*5*	*6*	*7*	*8*	*9*	*10*	*11*	*(0*
	4	*5*	*6*	*7*	*8*	*9*	*10*	*11*	*0*	*1*	*2*	*3*	*(4*

The original array of cyclic-intervals 5 and 8 is again converted into an array in the same mode, in a new key, and in the complementary interval system. Since odd and even sums are interchanged between the respective set forms of complementary cyclic intervals, the two arrays are not inversionally equivalent:

$$\begin{cases} p_4p_9/i_3p_{11} \\ i_3i_{10}/p_4i_8 \end{cases}$$

Analogous procedures applied to the tonic sum-tetrachords in the other partition of the original difference table will produce the same new arrays, i_5p_9/p_4p_{11} and p_4i_8/i_3i_{10}.

The two modulations in example 60 are effected, respectively, through an axis-interval transposition relative to a tonic cyclic chord and through a neighbor-interval transposition relative to a tonic sum-tetrachord. The passage quoted in the example gives special emphasis to cyclic-intervals 11,3 (=1,9), on which the entire movement is based, in that it is a progression of axis-dyad chords whose cyclic intervals are duplicated in another interval couple of the cyclic chord (i.e., interval-type axis-dyad chords):

```
     (bar 27)              (28)              (29)
p6p5:  5 0 6    5 0 6    3 2 4    3 2 4    1 4 2
i5i8:  8 0 5    6 2 3    6 2 3    4 4 1    4 4 1

                                  i3i2:  1 1 2    1 1 2
                                  p2p5:  4 1 1    2 3 11

(bar 30)                     (31)
   11 3 0   11 3 0   9 5 10    9 5 10    7 7 8    i3i0:  5 7 8
    2 3 11   0 5 9    0 5 9   10 7 7    10 7 7    p2p3:  8 7 7
```

EXAMPLE 60

Perle, Six Etudes, No. 1 (1973)

Copyright 1977 by Margun Music, Inc.
Used by permission.

Where the axis dyad is equivalent to a tonic sum the axis-dyad chords are simultaneously sum-type and interval-type, thus giving special emphasis to the tonic sums as well as to the cyclic intervals of the array. A shift in the axis dyad of the fifth chord effects a change to another array of the same mode. In the last two chords there is a second modulation, effected by reinterpreting the axis dyad of the penultimate chord in the example as a component of the last chord and transposing the neighbor interval of the common tonic sum-tetrachord. The cyclic elements of the last chord complete the sequential progression that commenced with the first chord in the example.

26. Imitative Counterpoint

Although, as Schoenberg points out, the twelve-tone row "functions in the manner of a motive,"[34] it is a fallacy to equate the Schoenbergian set and its basic transformations with thematic operations in tonal music, since the set, unlike the tonal theme, establishes the frame of reference, the context of tone relations, within which "themes" and "motives" are invented and manipulated. There is thus a problematical and ambiguous relation between the "thematic" and the "non-thematic." The priority of the perfect fifth and octave as intervals of imitation in a tonal fugue is inherent in the nature of the diatonic tonal system, whereas atonality provides no inherent criteria for the choice of one interval rather than another; the inversion or other literal transformation of a twelve-tone theme is a compositional possibility that is automatically given in the foundational premises of the system, whereas such thematic operations in diatonic tonality are elements of design that must be integrated and coordinated within the functional context of tonicity and triadic harmony.

The key- and mode-defining properties of cyclic sets, however, do not depend upon surface reiteration of linearly ordered sets of pitch classes. The relation between themes and their harmonic context in twelve-tone tonality is thus analogous, in a sense, to their relation in diatonic tonality. In twelve-tone, as in diatonic tonality, imitative counterpoint implies functional distinctions among intervals. The tritone, as well as the unison or octave, is a normative interval of imitation, since dyadic sums are unchanged at the tritone transposition. Thus the paired voices in strict imitation in the initial phrase of example 61 represent a characteristic relation of the system as a whole.

On the other hand, the imitation at $T(1)$ at the beginning of the second phrase reflects a specific property of Master Key 4. The two types of sum tetrachords produced by the sum alignment of an array will show the same difference between their respective aggregate sums as the cyclic intervals of that array. In Master Key 4, and in the modal representations of arrays that are semi-equivalent to those of Master Key 4, that difference is 4 and 8, as is implied in the key, 0,4, of the given array, $i_{11}i_6/p_{10}p_1$. Primary sum couples generate sum tetrachords in which the sum of secondary sums equals the sum of primary sums. For instance, in the following segment of the array secondary sum couple 8,4 coincides with

34. Schoenberg, *op. cit.*, p. 219.

EXAMPLE 61

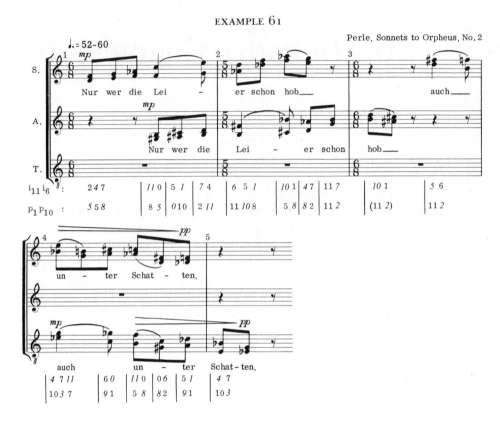

Perle, Sonnets to Orpheus, No. 2

Copyright 1975 by Boelke-Bomart, Inc.
Used by permission.

primary sum couple 1,11, each of which exhibits an aggregate sum of 0. In order to transpose from a sum tetrachord of one type to a sum tetrachord of the other type, the difference between the secondary sums of each must equal the difference between the primary sums of the other. The two segments of the sum table that comprise these transpositionally related tetrachords are shown below (Table 53). The secondary dyads of pitch-classes 5,11 (sum 4) and 2,6 (sum 8) in the first column of the first segment are respectively replaced by the primary dyads of pitch-classes 6,0 (sum 6) and 3,7 (sum 10) in the first column of the second segment; the primary dyads of 5,6 (sum 11) and 11,2 (sum 1) in the first column of the first segment are respectively replaced by 6,7 (sum 1) and 0,3 (sum 3) in the first column of the second segment; and so on for the remaining correspondingly ordered columns of the two segments of the array.

TABLE 53

	5	6	7	8	9	10	11	0	1	2	3	4	(5
Sum 4:	11	10	9	8	7	6	5	4	3	2	1	0	(11

	2	3	4	5	6	7	8	9	10	11	0	1	(2
Sum 8:	6	5	4	3	2	1	0	11	10	9	8	7	(6

	3	4	5	6	7	8	9	10	11	0	1	2	(3
Sum 3:	0	11	10	9	8	7	6	5	4	3	2	1	(0

	6	7	8	9	10	11	0	1	2	3	4	5	(6
Sum 1:	7	6	5	4	3	2	1	0	11	10	9	8	(7

Conversely, sum tetrachords whose secondary sums add up to 4 (the sum of primary sums 6 and 10) and show a difference of 10 or 2 (the difference between the opposite pair of primary sums, 11 and 1) are transposable at T(11) by reversing the operations described above.

Similarly, the content of each sum tetrachord of the following segment of the array, derived from the alignment of p_{10} and i_6 adjacencies,

	9	10	11	0	1	2	3	4	5	6	7	8	(9
Sum 7:	10	9	8	7	6	5	4	3	2	1	0	11	(10

	8	9	10	11	0	1	2	3	4	5	6	7	(8
Sum 9:	1	0	11	10	9	8	7	6	5	4	3	2	(1

is repeated at T(2) when the secondary sums 7 and 9 are respectively replaced by the primary sums 11 and 1, or when the primary sums 10 and 6 are respectively replaced by the secondary sums 2 and 10. These replacements are given in the following alignment of i_{11} and p_1 adjacencies:

	11	0	1	2	3	4	5	6	7	8	9	10	(11
Sum 2:	3	2	1	0	11	10	9	8	7	6	5	4	(3

	10	11	0	1	2	3	4	5	6	7	8	9	(10
Sum 10:	0	11	10	9	8	7	6	5	4	3	2	1	(0

The "minor third" has a special function as an interval of imitation wherever the tritone serves as an axis interval or as one of the characteristic intervals of a series of sum tetrachords. The +3 and −3 transpositions of an axis-note dyad respectively entail the −3 and +3 transpositions of its neighbor-note dyads. But the +3 and −3 transpositions of an interval-6 axis dyad are equivalent to each other in pitch-class content. Thus the axis-dyad chord or the sum tetrachord may be transposed as a whole by T(9) or T(3) within the given array.

The strict double canon by inversion in the first three bars of example 62 is premised on the fact that the two set forms of the array are inversionally complementary to each other. Such totally self-invertible arrays are always members of or semi-equivalent to members of Master Array 0.

EXAMPLE 62

In *any* array, paired sum scales will both be even or both be odd wherever a sum of adjacency sums is even, and any sum tetrachord generated by such paired sum scales will be invertible within the same sum-scale alignment. In the above alignment of sum-scales 8 and 4, for example, the first column is invertible in the sixth and twelfth columns, the second column in the fifth and eleventh columns, etc. But since the alignment of sum-scales 3 and 1 transposes the pitch-class content of each column of the former alignment, it must be inversionally related to it as well.

Cyclic chords, unlike sum tetrachords, are invertible and transposable at all pitch levels, since all combinations of the two cyclic intervals occur in the array.

27. Large-Scale Progression

We have shown (pp. 59ff.) how a progression through a series of arrays that share a single set form may be interpreted as a large-scale unfolding of that set form. Both mode and key change from array to array, but there is nevertheless a high degree of relatedness among all the arrays of such a progression, since the adjacency sums of the shared set form will be components of every array. A common mode or key, rather than a shared set form, may also serve as a basis for the association of various arrays. In example 63 $i_{11}p_7/p_4p_5$ is followed by another array of the same interval system (8,1) and mode (7,2): p_0i_8/i_5i_6. Cyclic chords of sum-couple 0,7 are tonic chords in both arrays, as neighbor notes of sum-4 axis dyads in the first array and sum-6 axis dyads in the second. The respective axis *interval* of identical tonic cyclic chords is the same in both arrays. The corresponding tonic segments of the two arrays are illustrated in Tables 54 and 55. The asterisks call attention to identical rows of pitch classes and show that each axis dyad doubles an element of its cyclic chord.

TABLE 54

Sum 0:	3	4	5	6	7	8	9	10	11	0	1	2	(3
	9	8	7	6	5	4	3	2	1	0	11	10	(9
Sum 4:	8	9	10	11	0	1	2	3	4	5	6	7	(8
	*8	7	6	5	4	3	2	1	0	11	10	9	(8
Sum 7:	11	0	1	2	3	4	5	6	7	8	9	10	(11
	*8	7	6	5	4	3	2	1	0	11	10	9	(8

TABLE 55

Sum 0:	3	4	5	6	7	8	9	10	11	0	1	2	(3
	*9	8	7	6	5	4	3	2	1	0	11	10	(9
Sum 6:	9	10	11	0	1	2	3	4	5	6	7	8	(9
	*9	8	7	6	5	4	3	2	1	0	11	10	(9
Sum 7:	11	0	1	2	3	4	5	6	7	8	9	10	(11
	8	7	6	5	4	3	2	1	0	11	10	0	(8

The two arrays of example 63 are part of a family of four arrays of cyclic-intervals 8 and 1 and mode 7,2 that share tonic cyclic chords of

EXAMPLE 63

Perle, Seventh Quartet, III (1973)

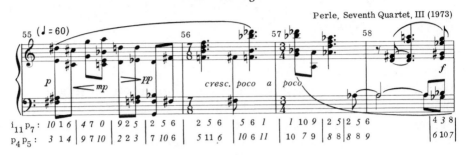

$i_{11}p_7$:   10 1 6 | 4 7 0 | 9 2 5 | 2 5 6 | 2 5 6 | 5 6 1 | 1 10 9 | 2 5 | 2 5 6   4 3 8

p_4p_5:   3 1 4 | 9 7 10 | 2 2 3 | 7 10 6 | 5 11 6 | 10 6 11 | 10 7 9 | 8 8 | 8 8 9   6 10 7

5 2 9 | 1 6 | 0 7 | 2 5 6 | 9 2 5 | 1 10 9 | 2 9 10 | 3 8 11 ‖ p_0i_8: 11 1 7 | 5 7 1 | 10 2 6 | 3 5 7

5 11 6 | 10 7 | 10 7 | 8 8 9 | 6 11 5 | 6 10 7 | 7 9 8 | 8 8 9 i_5i_6: 4 1 5 | 10 7 11 | 3 2 4 | 8 10 7

3 5 7   5 7 1   1 11 9 | 2 6 | 2 6 6   4 4 8 | 5 3 9 | 2 6 | 1 7 | 2 6 6

6 11 7   10 7 11   10 8 9 | 8 9 | 8 9 9   6 11 7 | 5 0 6 | 11 7 | 10 8 | 8 9 9

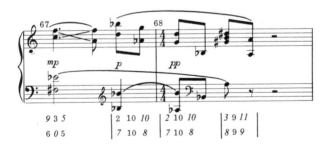

9 3 5   2 10 10 | 2 10 10 | 3 9 11

6 0 5   7 10 8 | 7 10 8 | 8 9 9

Copyright 1977 by Boelke-Bomart, Inc.
Used by permission.

sum-couple 0,7. In all four arrays the respective axis interval of identical tonic cyclic chords is the same, but for each array the pitch level of the tonic axis dyads is changed. Thus, relative to the first array, the series of axis dyads occurs at $T(1)$ in the second array, at $T(3)$ in p_2i_{10}/i_7i_8 (Table 56), and at $T(7)$ in $p_6i_2/i_{11}i_0$ (Table 57). The last array is a $T(3)$ transposition of the second, in that each of its adjacency sums differs from the corresponding adjacency sum of the second array (p_0i_8/i_5i_6) by 6. Since keys show the sums of aligned adjacencies of paired set forms, and the paired adjacencies of the last array will show a difference of $2\times6(=0)$ from the corresponding aligned adjacencies of the second array, both arrays will be in the same key, as well as the same mode (Table 58).

TABLE 56

Sum 0:	3	4	5	6	7	8	9	10	11	0	1	2	(3
	9	8	7	6	5	4	3	2	1	0	11	10	(9
Sum 10:	*11	0	1	2	3	4	5	6	7	8	9	10	(11
	11	10	9	8	7	6	5	4	3	2	1	0	(11
Sum 7:	*11	0	1	2	3	4	5	6	7	8	9	10	(11
	8	7	6	5	4	3	2	1	0	11	10	9	(8

TABLE 57

Sum 0:	*3	4	5	6	7	8	9	10	11	0	1	2	(3
	9	8	7	6	5	4	3	2	1	0	11	10	(9
Sum 6:	*3	4	5	6	7	8	9	10	11	0	1	2	(3
	3	2	1	0	11	10	9	8	7	6	5	4	(3
Sum 7:	11	0	1	2	3	4	5	6	7	8	9	10	(11
	8	7	6	5	4	3	2	1	0	11	10	9	(8

TABLE 58

	p_0i_8		p_6i_2	
	i_5i_6		$i_{11}i_0$	
Mode:	7,2	Mode:	7,2	

	p_0i_8		p_6i_2	
	i_6i_5		i_0i_{11}	
Key:	6,1	Key:	6,1	

If the sum, rather than the interval, of the respective axis dyads of identical cyclic chords is preserved, and if the axis dyads are again aligned to produce pitch-class doublings with cyclic elements, the original array, $i_{11}p_7/p_4p_5$, will be associated with three other arrays of the same *key* (4,11), rather than the same mode. The following additional arrays are generated: p_0i_8/i_3i_4 (Table 59), p_8i_4/i_7i_8 (Table 60), $p_4i_0/i_{11}i_0$ (Table 61).

TABLE 59

```
         3   4   5   6    7    8    9   10   11    0    1    2   (3
Sum 0:
        *9   8   7   6    5    4    3    2    1    0   11   10   (9

         7   8   9  10   11    0    1    2    3    4    5    6   (7
Sum 4:
        *9   8   7   6    5    4    3    2    1    0   11   10   (9

        11   0   1   2    3    4    5    6    7    8    9   10  (11
Sum 7:
         8   7   6   5    4    3    2    1    0   11   10    9   (8
```

TABLE 60

```
         3   4   5   6    7    8    9   10   11    0    1    2   (3
Sum 0:
         9   8   7   6    5    4    3    2    1    0   11   10   (9

       *11   0   1   2    3    4    5    6    7    8    9   10  (11
Sum 4:
         5   4   3   2    1    0   11   10    9    8    7    6   (5

       *11   0   1   2    3    4    5    6    7    8    9   10  (11
Sum 7:
         8   7   6   5    4    3    2    1    0   11   10    9   (8
```

TABLE 61

```
        *3   4   5   6    7    8    9   10   11    0    1    2   (3
Sum 0:
         9   8   7   6    5    4    3    2    1    0   11   10   (9

        *3   4   5   6    7    8    9   10   11    0    1    2   (3
Sum 4:
         1   0  11  10    9    8    7    6    5    4    3    2   (1

        11   0   1   2    3    4    5    6    7    8    9   10  (11
Sum 7:
         8   7   6   5    4    3    2    1    0   11   10    9   (8
```

With the exception of p_0i_8 and i_7i_8, each of which participates in two arrays, there are no duplications among the set forms that generate these seven arrays. In each array, however, either i_{11} or i_8 occurs as a component of one of the two set forms. From each of these tonic adjacency sums a set form that combines both cyclic intervals may be derived, and these cognate-related derived set forms will unfold the tonic cyclic chords shared by all seven arrays:

```
i₁₁:  |8  11 |0)  0||11   8||3   9||2   5||6  (6||5   2|  ||
        |7  0 |11   1||10   9||2  10||1   6||5   7||4  3||8  4|(7   0|
```

i_8 : |11 8|0) 0| |8 11| |9 3| |5 2| |6 (6| 2 5| ‖

|0 7 |1 11| |9 10| |10 2| |6 1| |7 5| |3 4| |4 8| |(0 7|

Each array may be similarly associated with other families of arrays of the same mode or key through tonic cyclic chords represented by sum scales other than 0 and 7. For example, the second array of example 63, p_0i_8/i_5i_6, shares tonic cyclic chords of sum-couple 8,1 with i_1p_9/p_6p_7. Where axis-sum 5 generates these chords in the former array, axis-sum 7 will generate them in the latter (Tables 62 and 63). Since the new array is a T(1) transposition, i_1p_9/p_6p_7, of the first array in example 63, $i_{11}p_7/p_4p_5$, it will be related to a T(1) transposition, p_2i_{10}/i_7i_8, of the second array, p_0i_8/i_5i_6, through a T(1) transposition of the cyclic chords of sum couple 0,7, as follows (cf. p. 137, above): i_1p_9/p_6p_7 (Table 64), p_2i_{10}/i_7i_8 (Table 65). The four arrays form part of a cycle whose continuation will eventually lead to a return of the initial array, as shown in Table 66. The groups of sum scales that comprise the tonic cyclic chords shared by successive arrays are shown at the left and right.

TABLE 62

Sum 8:	*7	8	9	10	11	0	1	2	3	4	5	6	(7
	1	0	11	10	9	8	7	6	5	4	3	2	(1
Sum 5:	*7	8	9	10	11	0	1	2	3	4	5	6	(7
	10	9	8	7	6	5	4	3	2	1	0	11	(10
Sum 1:	8	9	10	11	0	1	2	3	4	5	6	7	(8
	5	4	3	2	1	0	11	10	9	8	7	6	(5

TABLE 63

Sum 8:	7	8	9	10	11	0	1	2	3	4	5	6	(7
	1	0	11	10	9	8	7	6	5	4	3	2	(1
Sum 7:	*8	9	10	11	0	1	2	3	4	5	6	7	(8
	11	10	9	8	7	6	5	4	3	2	1	0	(11
Sum 1:	*8	9	10	11	0	1	2	3	4	5	6	7	(8
	5	4	3	2	1	0	11	10	9	8	7	6	(5

TABLE 64

Sum 2:	4	5	6	7	8	9	10	11	0	1	2	3	(4
	10	9	8	7	6	5	4	3	2	1	0	11	(10
Sum 6:	9	10	11	0	1	2	3	4	5	6	7	8	(9
	*9	8	7	6	5	4	3	2	1	0	11	10	(9
Sum 9:	0	1	2	3	4	5	6	7	8	9	10	11	(0
	*9	8	7	6	5	4	3	2	1	0	11	10	(9

TABLE 65

Sum 2:	*4*	*5*	*6*	*7*	*8*	*9*	*10*	*11*	*0*	*1*	*2*	*3*	*(4*
	*10	9	8	7	6	5	4	3	2	1	0	11	(10
Sum 8:	*10*	*11*	*0*	*1*	*2*	*3*	*4*	*5*	*6*	*7*	*8*	*9*	*(10*
	*10	9	8	7	6	5	4	3	2	1	0	11	(10
Sum 9:	*0*	*1*	*2*	*3*	*4*	*5*	*6*	*7*	*8*	*9*	*10*	*11*	*(0*
	9	8	7	6	5	4	3	2	1	0	11	10	(9

TABLE 66

$$
\begin{array}{ccc}
0 & & \\
4 & i_{11}p_7/p_4p_5 & \\
7 & & \\[4pt]
0 & & 8 \\
6 & p_0i_8/i_5i_6 & 5 \\
7 & & 1 \\[4pt]
2 & & 8 \\
6 & i_1p_9/p_6p_7 & 7 \\
9 & & 1 \\[4pt]
2 & & 10 \\
8 & p_2i_{10}/i_7i_8 & 7 \\
9 & & 3 \\[4pt]
4 & & 10 \\
8 & i_3p_{11}/p_8p_9 & 9 \\
11 & & 3 \\[4pt]
4 & & 0 \\
10 & p_4i_0/i_9i_{10} & 9 \\
11 & & 5 \\[4pt]
6 & & 0 \\
10 & i_5p_1/p_{10}p_{11} & 11 \\
1 & & 5 \\[4pt]
\text{etc.} & &
\end{array}
$$

Where a T(3) transposition $(i_5p_1/p_{10}p_{11})$ is reached after six steps in the above progression, we showed earlier (p. 139) how the same transposition may also be reached in a single step. Whatever the substitutions through which any array is converted into a second array, these may always be repeated to generate a series of arrays that returns to its point of origin. For the large-scale design of a composition, the structural implications of such closed cycles of arrays are analogous to the structural implications of relations among keys in the diatonic tonal system.

28. The Three Tonalities

We classify every dyad as a member of one or the other of two mutually exclusive categories, one of even and the other of odd pitch-class sums. Within each category symmetrically related dyads have the same sum and are respectively equivalent by transposition to the dyads of the remaining sums. Analogous generalizations apply to sum tetrachords, with the difference that the axis of symmetry of a sum tetrachord is expressed in the relation between two dyads, rather than two pitch classes.

Where a tetrachordal sum is even we find its symmetrically related dyadic sums by dividing the tetrachordal sum by 2. The division will give us a repeated even or a repeated odd integer, which we interpret as standing for a repeated dyadic sum. Let us assume, for example, that we have tetrachords of primary sum-couple 11,5. A division of the tetrachordal sum by 2 gives us the repeated integer 2 or 8. In any sum table that comprises sum tetrachords whose combined primary dyads give us a sum of 4, two sum-2 scales will be paired in one part of the array and two sum-8 scales in another part. The same sum tetrachords will be found in the difference table of the semi-equivalent array, in an alignment of complementary difference scales. Tetrachords of primary-sums 11 and 5 will unfold as follows in these segments of the respective arrays:

Sum 2:	*1*	*2*	*3*	.	.	.		Diff. 9:	*1*	*2*	*3*	.	.	.
	1	0	11						*4*	*5*	*6*			

Sum 2:	*4*	*5*	*6*	.	.	.		Diff. 3:	1	0	11	.	.	.
	10	9	8						10	9	8			

Sum 8:	*4*	*5*	*6*	.	.	.		Diff. 3:	*4*	*5*	*6*	.	.	.
	4	3	2						*1*	*2*	*3*			

Sum 8:	*1*	*2*	*3*	.	.	.		Diff. 9:	4	3	2	.	.	.
	7	6	5						7	6	5			

If the tetrachordal sum of 4 is given by primary sum-couple 0,4, the same sum scales and their corresponding difference tables will unfold as follows:

Sum 2:	*1*	*2*	*3*	.	.	.
	1	0	11			

Diff. 10:	*1*	*2*	*3*	.	.	.
	3	4	5			

Sum 2:	*3*	*4*	*5*	.	.	.
	11	10	9			

Diff. 2:	1	0	11	.	.	.
	11	10	9			

Sum 8:	*4*	*5*	*6*	.	.	.
	4	3	2			

Diff. 4:	*4*	*5*	*6*	.	.	.
	0	1	2			

Sum 8:	*0*	*1*	*2*	.	.	.
	8	7	6			

Diff. 8:	4	3	2	.	.	.
	8	7	6			

Every primary sum couple whose aggregate sum is 4 will give us another alignment of the same pairs of sum scales, and corresponding to each of these will be another pair of complementary difference scales. Where the primary sum couple is 2,2, the two sum-2 scales intersect at interval 0 and the corresponding difference scales are both of interval 0:

Sum 2:	*1*	*2*	*3*	.	.	.
	1	0	11			

Diff. 0:	*1*	*2*	*3*	.	.	.
	1	*2*	*3*			

Sum 2:	*1*	*2*	*3*	.	.	.
	1	0	11			

Diff. 0:	1	0	11	.	.	.
	1	0	11			

Sum 8:	*4*	*5*	*6*	.	.	.
	4	3	2			

Diff. 6:	*4*	*5*	*6*	.	.	.
	10	*11*	*0*			

Sum 8:	*10*	*11*	*0*	.	.	.
	10	9	8			

Diff. 6:	4	3	2	.	.	.
	10	9	8			

Similarly, where the primary sum couple is 8,8, the two sum-8 scales intersect at interval 0 and the corresponding difference scales are both of interval 0:

Sum 2:	*1*	2	*3*	.	.	.
	1	0	11			

Diff. 6:	*1*	*2*	*3*	.	.	.
	7	*8*	*9*			

Sum 2:	*7*	*8*	*9*	.	.	.
	7	6	5			

Diff. 6:	1	0	11	.	.	.
	7	6	5			

Sum 8:	*4*	*5*	*6*	.	.	.
	4	3	2			

Diff. 0:	*4*	*5*	*6*	.	.	.
	4	*5*	*6*			

Sum 8:	*4*	*5*	*6*	.	.	.
	4	3	2			

Diff. 0:	4	3	2	.	.	.
	4	3	2			

Thus **the seven collections of tetrachords whose primary sum couples form tetrachordal sums of 4 intersect at two of these collections, those of primary sum-couples 2,2 and 8,8. These are complementary to each** other and transpositionally equivalent at the "minor 3rd." We can read all these relations in the third and ninth columns of the table of Even Sums and Intervals (p. 17) by merely reinterpreting each pitch-class number as a dyadic sum and by assuming transpositional equivalence between complementary sum couples at $T(3)$ and $T(9)$ rather than at $T(6)$. **Collections of tetrachords whose primary sum couples form tetrachordal sums of 0 are merely transpositions of the sum-4 tetrachordal collections at $T(2)$, $T(5)$, $T(8)$, and $T(11)$, and those whose primary sum couples form tetrachordal sums of 8 are transpositions of the sum-4 tetrachordal collections at $T(1)$, $T(4)$, $T(7)$, and $T(10)$. All are in what we will call "Tonality 0."**

Where the tetrachordal sum is odd the dyadic sums at the axis of symmetry are n and $n\pm 1$. We can read each of these collections in the columns of the table of Odd Sums and Intervals (p. 17), by reinterpreting each pitch-class number as a dyadic sum. Let us assume that the tetrachordal sum is 1. In any sum table that comprises tetrachords of this sum, the sum scales at one point of intersection are 0 and 1, the sum scales at the other point of intersection are 6 and 7. Tetrachords of primary sum-couple 3,10, for example, will unfold as follows in these segments of the sum table and in the corresponding segments of the difference table of the semi-equivalent array:

Sum 0:	*0*	*1*	*2*	·	·	·		Diff. 2:	*0*	*1*	*2*	·	·	·
	0	11	10						*10*	*11*	*0*			

Sum 1:	*10*	*11*	*0*	·	·	·		Diff. 9:	*0*	*11*	*10*	·	·	·
	3	2	1						3	2	1			

Sum 6:	*3*	*4*	*5*	·	·	·		Diff. 8:	*3*	*4*	*5*	·	·	·
	3	2	1						7	8	9			

Sum 7:	*7*	*8*	*9*	·	·	·		Diff. 3:	*3*	*2*	*1*	·	·	·
	0	11	10						0	11	10			

Tetrachords of primary sum-couple 9,4 will be transpositionally equivalent to the preceding at $T(3)$ and $T(9)$, but not inversionally equivalent, since the sum of complementation would be odd ($3+4=10+9=7$), thereby interchanging even and odd primary sums.

Sum 6:	*3*	*4*	*5*	·	·	·		Diff. 2:	*3*	*4*	*5*	·	·	·
	3	2	1						*1*	*2*	*3*			

Sum 7:	*1*	*2*	*3*	·	·	·		Diff. 9:	*3*	*2*	*1*	·	·	·
	6	5	4						6	5	4			

Sum 0:	*0*	*1*	*2*	·	·	·		Diff. 8:	*0*	*1*	*2*	·	·	·
	0	11	10						4	5	6			

Sum 1:	*4*	*5*	*6*	·	·	·		Diff. 3:	*0*	*11*	*10*	·	·	·
	9	8	7						9	8	7			

The tetrachords of primary sum-couple 1,0 provide one axis of symmetry for the collections of sum-1 tetrachords:

	0	*1*	*2* . . .			*0*	*1*	*2* . . .
Sum 0:	0	11	10		Diff. 0:	0	1	2

	0	*1*	*2* . . .			*0*	*11*	*10* . . .
Sum 1:	1	0	11		Diff. 11:	1	0	11

	3	*4*	*5* . . .			*3*	*4*	*5* . . .
Sum 6:	3	2	1		Diff. 6:	9	10	11

	9	*10*	*11* . . .			*3*	*2*	*1* . . .
Sum 7:	10	9	8		Diff. 5:	10	9	8

The tetrachords of primary sum-couple 7,6 are the T(3) and T(9) transpositions of the preceding, and provide the other axis of symmetry:

	3	*4*	*5* . . .			*3*	*4*	*5* . . .
Sum 6:	3	2	1		Diff. 0:	3	4	5

	3	*4*	*5* . . .			*3*	*2*	*1* . . .
Sum 7:	4	3	2		Diff. 11:	4	3	2

	0	*1*	*2* . . .			*0*	*1*	*2* . . .
Sum 0:	0	11	10		Diff. 6:	6	7	8

	6	*7*	*8* . . .			*0*	*11*	*10* . . .
Sum 1:	7	6	5		Diff. 5:	7	6	5

Collections of tetrachords whose primary sum couples form tetrachordal sums of 5 are transpositions of the sum-1 tetrachordal collections at T(1), T(4), T(7), and T(10); collections of tetrachords whose primary sum couples form tetrachordal sums of 9 are transpositions of the sum-1 collections at T(2), T(5), T(8), and T(11). The remaining odd tetrachordal sums—3, 7, and 11—are inversional complements of the sum-1, sum-5, and sum-9 collections. All six aggregate collections of odd tetrachordal sums are classified as members of "Tonality 1."

There remain, finally, the even tetrachordal sums whose division by 2 generates a repeated odd integer. All of these are classified as components of "Tonality 2." Let us assume that the tetrachordal sum is 2. The collections of tetrachords of primary sum-couple 1,1 will give us an axis of symmetry for all sum-2 tetrachordal collections:

	0	*1*	*2* . . .			*0*	*1*	*2* . . .
Sum 1:	1	0	11		Diff. 0:	0	1	2

	0	*1*	*2* . . .			*1*	*0*	*11* . . .
Sum 1:	1	0	11		Diff. 0:	1	0	11

The collection of tetrachords of primary sum-couple 7,7 will give us the "minor 3rd" transposition of the same axis of symmetry:

Sum 7:	*3* *4* *5* . . .			Diff. 0:	*3* *4* *5* . . .		
	4 3 2				*3* *4* *5* . . .		

Sum 7:	*3* *4* *5* . . .	Diff. 0:	4 3 2 . . .
	4 3 2		4 3 2

In example 64 the successive arrays are derived from the progression to their axis of symmetry of tetrachordal collections whose different primary sum couples produce the same aggregate sum. The passage commences with a return to the opening bars, which are then redirected to bring the piece to a close. The tetrachordal sums in the key of the first array, p_0i_4/i_9p_{11}, are 11 and 1. Both collections of sum tetrachords are thus in Tonality 1. Sum 11 is given by the intersecting primary sum couple, 0,11, and this is preserved in each of the following arrays. The second tetrachordal sum is successively represented by primary sum couples 4,9; 3,10; 2,11; and 1,0. The successive arrays thus converge upon the axis of symmetry, 1,0, of the collections of sum-1 tetrachords. Each array is in another interval system, successively 4,2; 3,1; 2,0; and 1,11. The same series of sum scales appears in all four arrays, since the tetrachordal sums, 11 and 1, are the same:

$$10 \quad 1 \quad 0 \quad 11 \quad 2 \quad 9 \quad 4 \quad 7 \quad 6 \quad 5 \quad 8 \quad 3 \quad (10$$

Each pair of scales that generates sum-11 tetrachords preserves the same setting in all four arrays, since the primary sum couple, 0,11, is the same. Each pair is shifted relative to its neighboring pair, however, in order to change the settings that generate sum-1 tetrachords. We illustrate these changes below with a segment of each array (Table 67).

TABLE 67

p_0i_4/i_9p_{11},		$p_0p_3/p_{10}p_{11}$,		$p_0i_2/i_{11}p_{11}$,		p_0p_1/p_0p_{11},	
Sum 11:	*0* *1* 11 10	Sum 11:	*0* *1* 11 10	Sum 11:	*0* *1* 11 10	Sum 11:	*0* *1* 11 10
Sum 0:	*0* *1* 0 11	Sum 0:	*0* *1* 0 11	Sum 0:	*0* *1* 0 11	Sum 0:	*0* *1* 0 11
Sum 1:	*4* *5* 9 8	Sum 1:	*3* *4* 10 9	Sum 1:	*2* *3* 11 10	Sum 1:	*1* *2* 0 1
Sum 10:	*2* *3* 8 7	Sum 10:	*1* *2* 9 8	Sum 10:	*0* *1* 10 9	Sum 10:	*11* *0* 11 10

The final chord of example 64 has as its axis the tonic sum 0, as represented by the axis of symmetry of that dyadic sum, pitch classes

0,0. One of its neighbor-note dyads, pitch classes 0,11, is the same in all four arrays; the other is semitonally contracted each time to converge upon the final sum-1 dyad, pitch classes 1,0. Sum-scales 0 and 11 represent tonic sums in all four arrays, whereas sum-scale 1 represents a tonic sum only in the last array.

EXAMPLE 64

Perle, Six Etudes, No. 4 (1976)

Copyright 1977 by Margun Music, Inc.
Used by permission.

The three chords that are described in the preceding paragraph as converging upon the final chord are not actually exploited to bring the composition to a close. Instead, at corresponding points in the phrases that precede the closing bar (the third beat of bars 84, 86, and 88), the progression is realized in the successive transformation of a tetrachord given by sum-scales 3 and 10:

p_0i_4/i_9p_{11}, $p_0p_3/p_{10}p_{11}$, $p_0i_2/i_{11}p_{11}$,

Sum 10: $\begin{matrix} 8 \\ 2 \end{matrix}$ Sum 10: $\begin{matrix} 8 \\ 2 \end{matrix}$ Sum 10: $\begin{matrix} 8 \\ 2 \end{matrix}$

Sum 3: $\begin{matrix} 2 \\ 1 \end{matrix}$ Sum 3: $\begin{matrix} 1 \\ 2 \end{matrix}$ Sum 3: $\begin{matrix} 0 \\ 3 \end{matrix}$

Each phrase as a whole is analogously transformed to reflect the progression of arrays. A literal continuation in the last bar (ex. 65) would have led to the following sum tetrachord at the conclusion of the fourth array:

p_0p_1/p_0p_{11},

Sum 10: $\begin{matrix} 8 \\ 2 \end{matrix}$

Sum 3: $\begin{matrix} 11 \\ 4 \end{matrix}$

EXAMPLE 65

$\lfloor p_0p_1/p_0p_{11} \rfloor$

In place of this, and registrally displaced so that all four notes appear in the right hand part, there is another tetrachord of the same primary sum couple, 1,0—a tonic sum-tetrachord that uniquely characterizes the collection of such tetrachords, in that its secondary and tertiary sum couples are *both* identical with its primary sum couple:

p_0p_1/p_0p_{11},

Sum 0: $\begin{matrix} 0 \\ 0 \end{matrix}$

Sum 1: $\begin{matrix} 1 \\ 0 \end{matrix}$

The modulation from each array into the next is of a type which we have not described earlier. All four arrays share tetrachords of primary sum-couple 0,11; the alternate tetrachords of the sum tables share a single tetrachordal sum, but the latter is partitioned into a different primary sum couple in each array. We have shown above how one array is converted into another through shifts of one degree between adjacent pairs of the sum scales whose fixed settings generate the tetrachords of primary sum-couple 0,11. For each such shift, one neighbor-note dyad of any given axis dyad is retained, while the other neighbor-note dyad is replaced by an adjacent dyad of the same sum scale. Where the shift results in the substitution of interval 1 for interval 11 of the same sum, or vice versa, the pitch-class content of the neighbor-note dyad, and thus of the axis-dyad chord, is invariant between the two arrays. These intersections are the basis for modulation from each array into the next in example 64 (Table 68).

TABLE 68

$p_0i_4/i_9p_{11},$		$p_0p_3/p_{10}p_{11},$			$p_0i_2/i_{11}p_{11},$			$p_0p_1/p_0p_{11},$	
Sum 7:	$\begin{matrix}1\\6\end{matrix}$	Sum 7:	$\begin{matrix}1\\6\end{matrix}$	$\begin{matrix}2\\5\end{matrix}$	Sum 7:	$\begin{matrix}2\\5\end{matrix}$	$\begin{matrix}3\\4\end{matrix}$	Sum 7:	$\begin{matrix}3\\4\end{matrix}$
Sum 4:	$\begin{matrix}5\\11\end{matrix}$	Sum 4:	$\begin{matrix}5\\11\end{matrix}$	$\begin{matrix}6\\10\end{matrix}$	Sum 4:	$\begin{matrix}6\\10\end{matrix}$	$\begin{matrix}7\\9\end{matrix}$	Sum 4:	$\begin{matrix}7\\9\end{matrix}$
Sum 9:	$\begin{matrix}5\\4\end{matrix}$	Sum 9:	$\begin{matrix}4\\5\end{matrix}$	$\begin{matrix}5\\4\end{matrix}$	Sum 9:	$\begin{matrix}4\\5\end{matrix}$	$\begin{matrix}5\\4\end{matrix}$	Sum 9:	$\begin{matrix}4\\5\end{matrix}$

Similarly, a shift of two degrees will produce invariant neighbor-note dyads of interval 10/2 and result in intersecting axis-dyad chords between the first array and the third; and a shift of three degrees will produce invariant neighbor-note dyads of interval 3/9 and result in intersecting axis-dyad chords between the first array and the fourth. Examples are given in Tables 69 and 70.

TABLE 69

$p_0i_4/i_9p_{11},$		$p_0i_2/i_{11}p_{11},$	
Sum 6:	$\begin{matrix}2\\4\end{matrix}$	Sum 6:	$\begin{matrix}4\\2\end{matrix}$
Sum 7:	$\begin{matrix}0\\7\end{matrix}$	Sum 7:	$\begin{matrix}0\\7\end{matrix}$
Sum 4:	$\begin{matrix}4\\0\end{matrix}$	Sum 4:	$\begin{matrix}4\\0\end{matrix}$

TABLE 70

p_0i_4/i_9p_{11}, p_0p_1/p_0p_{11},

Sum 7: $\begin{matrix} 2 \\ 5 \end{matrix}$ Sum 7: $\begin{matrix} 2 \\ 5 \end{matrix}$

Sum 4: $\begin{matrix} 6 \\ 10 \end{matrix}$ Sum 4: $\begin{matrix} 6 \\ 10 \end{matrix}$

Sum 9: $\begin{matrix} 6 \\ 3 \end{matrix}$ Sum 9: $\begin{matrix} 3 \\ 6 \end{matrix}$

29. Triadic Arrays

In the preceding section we have shown that every tetrachordal sum may be construed in terms of its component dyads, and that these may be read from the basic array of sums and intervals (p. 17) by reinterpreting each pitch class number of the latter as a dyadic sum. The same array is useful as a guide to the implications of triadic collections as well.

All the dyadic collections of the basic array may be converted into triadic collections of a single sum by the addition of a third pitch class number: n to each dyad of sum 0, $n-2$ to each dyad of sum 2, $n-4$ to each dyad of sum 4, and so on for each column in the table of Even Sums and Intervals; $n-1$ to each dyad of sum 1, $n-3$ to each dyad of sum 3, and so on for each column in the table of Odd Sums and Intervals. Let us assume, for example, that we wish to generate all triadic collections of sum 2. The addition of pitch-class 9 ($=2-5$) to each dyad of sum 5 converts the third column of the table of Odd Sums and Intervals into a sub-collection of sum-2 triads (Table 71).

TABLE 71

9,3,2

9,4,1

9,5,0

9,6,11

9,7,10

9,8,9

Each of these occurs in two other orderings elsewhere in the collection of sum-2 triads. For example, 2,3,9 is found by the addition of pitch-class 2 the sum-0 column, and 3,9,2 by the addition of 3 to the sum-11 column. We can convert the original table of even dyadic sums into a table of all the even triadic sums exclusively, by the successive addition of each even pitch-class number in turn, and into a table of all the odd triadic sums by the successive addition of each odd pitch-class number in turn. Where the original tables generate 42 different even and 36 different odd dyadic collections, the triadic tables generate 182 different even and 182 different odd triadic collections.

The principle of inversional complementation as a basis of set structure has meant, until now, the alignment of P and I cycles in a one-to-one relation, to generate a complete collection of symmetrically related dyads for each such alignment. Any dyadic cyclic set form will be derivable from one or another column of the table of dyadic sums and differences. For example, from the sum-5 column we derive $i_5 i_6$ by reading down from left to right, $p_5 p_4$ by reading up from left to right, the two partitions of $i_5 p_7$ by reading down from left to right and omitting every other dyad, and so on. (The ninth column of the same table is, of course, a continuation of the third and must be employed as such in performing these operations.)

Analogous readings of the same column in its above conversion to triadic sum 2 will similarly generate set forms of three cyclic intervals. The successive dyadic sums of the original column differ by 0 and we convert them into triads of a single sum by the addition of a complementary cycle of interval 0. Reading alternate triads from left to right in descending order, for example, we may interpret the overlapping cyclic intervals as P-0 (or I-0), P-2, I-2. From the same column we derive another partition, and from each of the other eleven non-equivalent columns, correspondingly converted according to our formula to provide the same triadic sum, two more partitions of the same set form. Where an alternate segmentation of the dyadic set form produces a second collection of symmetrically related dyads (except where the cyclic interval is 0), alternate segmentations of the triadic set form produce two additional triadic sums. Thus, the above conversion of the third column to a set of sum-2 triads with cyclic intervals P-0, P-2, I-2 yields additional triadic sums of 2 and 4. For example:

$$9 \quad 3 \quad 2 \quad 9 \quad 5 \quad 0 \quad \ldots$$

A triadic set form that conforms to exactly the same conditions may be formed by the conversion of a row rather than a column of the original table. Reading from left to right, the successive sums of the given dyads differ by P-2. The added pitch classes will therefore be components of an I-2 cycle. The overlapping cyclic intervals of the triadic set may then be read as I-2, P-1, P-1. Our initial triad, 9,3,2, for example, would be a component of the following row of sum-2 triads:

1,1,0   11,2,1   9,3,2   7,4,3   5,5,4   3,6,5   1,7,6   11,8,7   . . .

Each of the other eleven rows of the original tables may be converted into one of the remaining partitions of the same set form. The latter may be identified by its ordered triadic sums, 2,0,1. If we wish to specify that the cyclic intervals are understood to be I-2, P-1, P-1, rather than the equivalent P-10, I-11, I-11, or I-2, P-1, I-11, or I-2, I-11, P-1, we may do so by assigning aspect names to the triadic sums: $i_2p_0i_1$.[35] We have purposely chosen as our first examples of triadic sets two that follow an obvious path through the converted master array of sums and intervals, unlike the following, in which cycles of I-5 and I-3 are complemented by P-8.

$i_0p_7p_4$:   4 6 2 11 3 *10* 6 0 6 1 9 2 8 6 *10* 3 3 6 10 0 2 5 9

10 0 6 *6* 7 3 2 2 0 *10* 9 9 6 (4 6 2

Any series of three pitch-class numbers whose sum is 0, 7, or 4, and which does not occur, identically ordered, as a triadic component of the above partition, may serve as the point of origin of another partition of the same set form.

Fundamental distinctions must be drawn between the properties of triadic and dyadic cyclic sets.

Every dyadic set form is equivalent to itself at the T(6) transposition, since the addition of 6 to each of two pitch-class numbers is equivalent to the addition of 0 to the dyadic sum. For triadic sets equivalence occurs at T(4) and T(8), since the addition of 4 to each pitch-class number, or of 8 to each pitch-class number, will revise the triadic sum by 0.

Two triadic set forms are transpositions of one another only where their respective sums differ by the same multiple of 3 and have the same aspect names, and inversions of one another only where the respective sums are complementary to the same multiple of 3 and have the opposite aspect names.

Although the retrograde statement of a cycle transforms it into its inversion, prime and retrograde aspects of dyadic sets are generated by the same cycles, since the two cycles are already inversionally complementary to each other. But of the three cycles of the triadic set, only two can be inversionally related, and such an inversionally complementary pair is not present unless the remaining cyclic interval is 0. Thus the cycles that generate the inversion also generate the retrograde of a given triadic set form, but the two aspects differ in the order of the cycles in respect to the original set form. The retrograde of the latter is generated by complementing the original cycles in their reversed respective order, the inversion by complementing them in their original order, and the retrograde-inversion by reversing the order of the original cycles. Thus the last triadic set discussed above, which was generated by I-5, I-3, P-8, changes its cycles to I-8, P-3, P-5 in the retrograde, to P-5, P-3, I-8 in the inversion, and to P-8, I-3, I-5 in the retrograde-inversion.

---

35. We can apply the aspect names consistently with what we did in naming dyadic sets by observing the following rule: to find the cycle determine the interval between adjacent numbers in the name of the set, subtracting the left from the right for even p or odd i sums, and vice versa for odd p or even i sums.

Presumably it would be possible to work out the implications of triadic sets in terms of analogies with dyadic sets, with their respective sum and difference tables, master modes and master keys, tonic and resultant set forms, derived sets, and so on. Compositional experience to date with triadic sets has not led in the direction of this intimidating prospect. A type of triadic array that has already proved compositionally meaningful is one that has no special significance for dyadic sets—the pairing of retrograde-related set forms. Since each cycle of a given triadic set form is replaced by its complement in the retrograded set form, the pairing of the two triadic set forms is equivalent to an alignment of three dyadic set forms. Any two of the latter will be identical with a dyadic array. Suppose, for example, that we pair the above partition of an I-5, I-3, P-8 set form with a retrograde of the same partition so that I-5 is vertically aligned with I-8, I-3 with P-3, and P-8 with P-5:

$i_0p_7p_4$: 4 6 2 11 3 *10* 6 0 6 1 9 2 8 6 *10* 3 3 6 . . .

$i_0p_4i_7$: 6 *9* 9 10 *0* 2 2 *3* 7 6 6 0 10 *9* 5 2 0 *10* . . .

Embedded in the above we find a difference alignment of a dyadic array of cyclic-intervals 5,8:

p_8p_1: 4 *9* 11   2 6   7 1   0 8   *5* 3   *10* . . .

p_0i_8: 6   2 *10* *10* 2   6 6   2 10 *10* 2   6 . . .

For this we can substitute any other segment of the difference table of p_8p_1/p_0i_8. All of them will be found in that segment of the triadic array in which the respective cycles are aligned as above and in which the vertical dyads of sum 3 are fixed by the same pitch classes of I-3 and P-3. We can easily convert the difference table of the dyadic array to show these partitions of the triadic array (Table 72). (The dyadic array is read in the usual way; the paired triadic partitions are found by reading down each column.)

In the following realignment of the same triadic partitions $i_0p_4i_7$ is shifted three places to the left relative to $i_0p_7p_4$. The same cycles are paired as in the original alignment, but the shift causes I-3 and P-3 to produce a new constant sum, 6 in place of 3, and generates a new component dyadic array in the same interval system, 5,8.

$i_0p_7p_4$: 4 6 2 11 3 *10* 6 0 6 1 9 2 8 6 *10* 3 3 6 . . .

$i_0p_4i_7$: 10 *0* 2 2 *3* 7 6 6 0 10 *9* 5 2 0 *10* 6 *3* 3 . . .

i_1i_6: 4 2 11   7 6 0 1 5 8 *10* 3 6 . . .

p_4i_0: 10 2 2 *10* 6 6 10 2 2 *10* 6 3 . . .

TABLE 72

Diff. 10:	4	3	2	1	0	11	10	9	8	7	6	5	(4
	6	5	4	3	2	1	0	11	10	9	8	7	(6

Sum 3:	9 --
	6 --

Diff. 5:	*2*	*3*	*4*	*5*	*6*	*7*	*8*	*9*	*10*	*11*	*0*	*1*	*(2*
	9	*10*	*11*	*0*	*1*	*2*	*3*	*4*	*5*	*6*	*7*	*8*	*(9*

Diff. 1:	11	10	9	8	7	6	5	4	3	2	1	0	(11
	10	9	8	7	6	5	4	3	2	1	0	11	(10

Sum 3:	0 --
	3 --

Diff. 8:	*10*	*·11*	*0*	*1*	*2*	*3*	*4*	*5*	*6*	*7*	*8*	*9*	*(10*
	2	*3*	*4*	*5*	*6*	*7*	*8*	*9*	*10*	*11*	*0*	*1*	*(2*

Diff. 4:	6	5	4	3	2	1	0	11	10	9	8	7	(6
	2	1	0	11	10	9	8	7	6	5	4	3	(2

Sum 3:	*3* --
	0 --

etc.

TABLE 73

KEY[36]	MODE	ARRAY
4,1	8,5	$p_8 p_1 / p_0 i_8$
1,10	9,6	$i_1 i_6 / p_4 i_0$
10,7	10,7	$p_6 p_{11} / p_8 i_4$
7,4	11,8	$i_{11} i_4 / p_0 i_8$
4,1	0,9	$p_4 p_9 / p_4 i_0$
1,10	1,10	$i_9 i_2 / p_8 i_4$
10,7	2,11	$p_2 p_7 / p_0 i_8$
7,4	3,0	$i_7 i_0 / p_4 i_0$
4,1	4,1	$p_0 p_5 / p_8 i_4$
1,10	5,2	$i_5 i_{10} / p_0 i_8$
10,7	6,3	$p_{10} p_3 / p_4 i_0$
7,4	7,4	$i_3 p_8 / p_8 i_4$
(4,1)	(8,5)	$(p_8 p_1 / p_0 i_8)$

36. We give the key of the dyadic array in order to distinguish in the usual way

A series of such realignments in the paired triadic partitions will generate a cycle of twelve component dyadic arrays in the same interval system. Each dyadic set form is successively transformed in terms of its own cyclic interval (Table 73).

Indeed, the difference tables of all 144 arrays of interval-system 5,8 will be found as components of the one triadic array, $i_0p_7p_4/i_0p_4i_7$. The following alignment, for example, in which the recurrent sum 3 is produced by new pitch classes of I-3 and P-3, preserves the original key, 4,1, of the dyadic array, but changes its mode:

| $i_0p_7p_4$: | 5 | 5 | 2 | 0 | 2 | *10* | 7 | 11 | *6* | 2 | 8 | 2 | 9 | 5 | *10* | 4 | 2 | 6 | . . . |
| $i_0p_4i_7$: | 5 | *10* | 9 | 9 | *1* | 2 | 1 | 4 | 7 | 5 | 7 | 0 | 9 | *10* | 5 | 1 | 1 | *10* | . . . |

| i_9i_2 : | 5 | | 9 | 0 | | 2 | 7 | | 7 | 2 | | 0 | 9 | | 5 | 4 | | *10* | . . . |
| $i_{11}p_7$: | 5 | | 2 | 9 | | *10* | 1 | | 6 | 5 | | 2 | 9 | | *10* | 1 | | 6 | . . . |

The following alignment preserves the original mode, 8,5, of the dyadic array, but changes the key. A new recurrent sum, 1, is produced by the paired I-3 and P-3 cycles, but the series of differences produced by their vertically aligned pitch classes is the same as it was in the original triadic alignment.

| $i_0p_7p_4$: | 5 | 5 | 2 | | 0 | | 2 | *10* | 7 | 11 | *6* | 2 | 8 | 2 | | 9 | 5 | *10* | 4 | | 2 | 6 | . . . |
| $i_0p_4i_7$: | 7 | 8 | 9 | | 11 | | *11* | 2 | 3 | 2 | 7 | 7 | 5 | 0 | | 11 | 8 | 5 | 3 | | *11* | 10 | . . . |

| i_9i_2: | 5 | | 9 | 0 | | 2 | 7 | | 7 | 2 | | 0 | 9 | | 5 | 4 | | *10* | . . . |
| i_1p_9: | 7 | | 2 | 11 | | *10* | 3 | | 6 | 7 | | 2 | 11 | | *10* | 3 | | 6 | . . . |

A shift of $3n+1$ places to the left in $i_0p_4i_7$ relative to $i_0p_7p_4$ rotates the sums of one in respect to the sums of the other and realigns the interval cycles as follows:

I-5   I-3   P-8

P-3   P-5   I-8

The component dyadic arrays will all be in interval-system 5,3. For example:

| $i_0p_7p_4$: | 4 | 6 | 2 | 11 | 3 | *10* | 6 | 0 | 6 | 1 | 9 | 2 | 8 | 6 | *10* | 3 | 3 | 6 | . . . |
| $p_4i_7i_0$: | 9 | 9 | 10 | 0 | 2 | 2 | *3* | 7 | 6 | 6 | 0 | 10 | 9 | 5 | 2 | 0 | *10* | 6 | . . . |

| p_8p_1: | 4 | *9* | | 11 | 2 | | 6 | 7 | | 1 | 0 | | 8 | 5 | | 3 | *10* | | . . . |
| i_6i_3: | 9 | 6 | | 0 | 3 | | 3 | 0 | | 6 | 9 | | 9 | 6 | | 0 | 3 | | . . . |

between different arrays in the same mode, although the sum tables of these dyadic arrays are not components of the given triadic array.

For the above segment of the p_8p_1/i_3i_6 array we may substitute any other sum alignment of the same array (Table 74).

TABLE 74

Sum 1:	9	10	11	0	1	2	3	4	5	6	7	8	(9
	4	3	2	1	0	11	10	9	8	7	6	5	(4

Sum 3:	9	10	11	0	1	2	3	4	5	6	7	8	(9
	6	5	4	3	2	1	0	11	10	9	8	7	(6

Sum 0: 2 ---
        10 --

Sum 11:	0	1	2	3	4	5	6	7	8	9	10	11	(0
	11	10	9	8	7	6	5	4	3	2	1	0	(11

Sum 5:	2	3	4	5	6	7	8	9	10	11	0	1	(2
	3	2	1	0	11	10	9	8	7	6	5	4	(3

Sum 0: 10 --
        2 ---

Sum 9:	3	4	5	6	7	8	9	10	11	0	1	2	(3
	6	5	4	3	2	1	0	11	10	9	8	7	(6

Sum 7:	7	8	9	10	11	0	1	2	3	4	5	6	(7
	0	11	10	9	8	7	6	5	4	3	2	1	(0

Sum 0: 6 ---
        6 ---

etc.

Procedures corresponding to those described above will generate, as components of the given rotation of the triadic array, every sum table of the 144 arrays of interval-system 5,3.

Finally, a shift of $3n$-1 places to the left in the original alignment of $i_0p_4i_7$ relative to $i_0p_7p_4$ realigns the interval cycles as follows:

$$\text{I-5} \quad \text{I-3} \quad \text{P-8}$$

$$\text{P-5} \quad \text{I-8} \quad \text{P-3}$$

The component dyadic arrays will all be in interval-system 3,8. For example:

$i_0p_7p_4$: 4 6 2 11 3 *10* 6 0 6 1 9 2 8 6 *10* 3 3 6 . . .

$i_7i_0p_4$: 9 10 *0* 2 2 *3* 7 6 6 0 10 9 5 2 *0* *10* 6 *3* . . .

i_3i_6:   6 *0*   3 *3*   0 6   9 9   6 *0*   3 *3* . . .

p_4i_0:   10 2   2 *10*   6 6   10 2   2 *10*   6 *6* . . .

The difference tables of all 144 arrays of interval-system 3,8 will be found as components of the same triadic array, where the respective triadic sums are aligned as in this last rotation.

In example 66 one of the above triadic set forms, $i_0p_7p_4$, is combined with an "unequal" transposition of the other. As we have pointed out above, in order to transpose a triadic set form we must add the same multiple of 3 to each of its triadic sums, if each pitch class is to be equally transposed. But the new set form, $i_8p_0i_3$, is "transposed" by the addition of 8 to each corresponding triadic sum of the former set form. Thus, for example, two elements of each triad in corresponding partitions of the two set forms may be transposed at T(3) and one element at T(2). Any other distribution of the same sum will produce another partition of $i_8p_0i_3$.

In the triadic array on which the example is based the cycles are aligned as follows:

$$p_4i_0p_7: \qquad \text{P-8} \quad \text{I-5} \quad \text{I-3}$$

$$i_8p_0i_3: \qquad \text{I-8} \quad \text{P-3} \quad \text{P-5}$$

The component dyadic arrays are thus all in interval-system 5,3. In the passage quoted the dyadic arrays are represented by sum tetrachords only, except at D and E, where there are axis-dyad chords. Each pair of dyads produced by the paired interval-8 cycles forms a second, symmetrical, tetrachord, which is shown in the lowest staff in the example. The recurring sum generated by the vertical alignment of these complementary cycles is indicated in the analysis that follows the example.

Where we are exploiting only the sum tetrachords of the dyadic component we can easily show the resources that are available relative to the recurring vertical sum. Any two elements of the P-8 cycle will enclose any dyad whose sum will complete the overlapping triadic sums 4 and 0; any two elements of the I-8 cycle will enclose any dyad whose sum will complete the overlapping triadic sums 8 and 0. The sum tetrachords that are available relative to the recurring vertical sum 4, for example, are all shown in Table 75. We will use letter names here for the elements of the P-8 and I-8 cycles and integers for the intervening dyadic sums. Each of the latter may be represented by *any* member of the collection of dyads symmetrical to that sum.

TABLE 75

$p_4i_0(p_7)$: d 2 $b\flat$ 6 $f\sharp$ 10 d

$i_8p_0(i_3)$: d 6 $f\sharp$ 2 $b\flat$ 10 d

f 11 $c\sharp$ 3 a 7 f b 5 g 9 $e\flat$ 1 b

b 9 $d\sharp$ 5 g 1 b f 3 a 11 $c\sharp$ 7 f

$g\sharp$ 8 e 0 c 4 $g\sharp$

$g\sharp$ 0 c 8 e 4 $g\sharp$

EXAMPLE 66

Perle, Songs of Praise and Lamentation, III (1974)

Copyright 1975 by Boelke-Bomart, Inc.
Used by permission.

A)

$p_4i_0p_7$:	7	10	11	*3*		*1*	1	2	9		*1*	4	11	9
$i_8p_0i_3$:	9	2	9	1		3	*11*	6	7		3	2	*3*	7

B) C)

sums: (4)   (4)   (4)   (4)   (4)   (4)

D)

7	*1*	11	4	9
2	3	*10*	7	7

(4)   (4)

E)

1	4	11	9	11
3	*3*	2	7	6

(4)   (4)

F)

0	11	5	*8*
2	2	4	6

(2)   (2)

G)

0	0	4	*8*
2	*3*	3	6

(2)   (2)

H)

6	0	10	2
8	9	3	0

(2)   (2)

I)

6	3	7	2
8	*0*	*0*	0

(2)   (2)

J)

6	1	9	2
8	*10*	2	0

(2)   (2)

K)

6	0	10	2
8	*9*	*3*	0

(2)   (2)

L)

0	4	*0*	8
2	7	*11*	6

(2)   (2)

M)

6	7	3	2
8	*10*	2	0

(2)   (2)

N)

6	1	9	2
8	*4*	*8*	0

(2)   (2)

O)

4	8	4	*0*
2	*6*	*0*	6

(6)   (6)

P)

4	9	3	*0*
2	7	*11*	6

(6)   (6)

Q)

6	8	2	2
4	*6*	*10*	8

(10)   (10)

R)

6	1	9	2
4	*11*	*5*	6

(10)   (10)

S)

10	11	7	*6*
8	*3*	9	0

(6)   (6)

T)

10	6	0	*6*
8	*10*	2	0

(6)   (6)

30. Conclusion

In the traditional tonal system every simultaneity and every progression is referable to a single type of chord structure, the triad, and to the complex of functional relations postulated in the concept of a "key center." There are no precompositional principles that comparably regulate simultaneity and progression in atonal music. "The 'rightness' of a particular note depends not upon its possible containment within a pre-established harmonic unit, as it does in tonality, but upon larger compositional factors whose meaning must be discovered within the work itself."[37] The term "reflexive reference" has been suggested to describe an analogous situation in modern poetry: "Since the primary reference of any word-group is to something inside the poem itself, language in modern poetry is really reflexive: the meaning-relationship is completed only by the simultaneous perception in space of word-groups which, when read consecutively in time, have no comprehensible relation to each other. Instead of the instinctive and immediate reference of words and word-groups to the objects or events they symbolize, and the construction of meaning from the sequence of these references, modern poetry asks its readers to suspend the process of individual reference temporarily until the entire pattern of internal references can be apprehended as a unity. This explanation, of course, is the extreme statement of an ideal condition rather than of an actually existing state of affairs; but the conception of poetic form that runs through Mallarmé to Pound and Eliot, and which has left its traces on a whole generation of modern poets, can be formulated only in terms of the principle of reflexive reference."[38]

As in modern poetry, "reflexive reference" is entirely relevant and sufficient only as an explanation of an ideal, rather than an actual, musical condition. The existence of something that we identify as the "Tristan chord" suggests that in tonal music, too, it sometimes happens that "the primary reference of [a given chord] is to something inside the [composition] itself;" in atonal music, on the other hand, there may be normative and precompositional, as well as reflexive, referential elements.

In Schoenberg's Opus 11, No. 1, the initial thematic idea (ex. 67) is varied in contour and relative pitch content upon its first restatement (ex. 68). Every such variant in a tonal composition may be explained in

37. Perle, *Serial Composition and Atonality,* p. 9.
38. Joseph Frank, "Spatial Form in Modern Literature," in *Criticism: The Foundations of Literary Judgment,* ed. by Mark Schorer *et al.* (New York, Chicago, Burlingame: Harcourt, Brace and World, 1958), p. 383.

terms of its harmonic meaning—a change in mode, a sequential shift that revises functional implications, and so on. A similarly non-reflexive explanation applies to example 68. A thematic idea that specifically appertains to the given composition is restated in terms of a general type of pitch-class collection.

EXAMPLE 67

Copyright 1910 by Universal Edition, A.G., Vienna.
Renewed 1938 by Arnold Schoenberg.
Used by permission of Belmont Music Publishers, Los Angeles.

EXAMPLE 68

Bars 9–10 unfold a five-note segment of one of the two whole-tone cycles plus one "odd," or "dissonant," note; the latter anticipates the change of harmony in bar 11 to a four-note segment of the alternative whole-tone cycle and "resolves" to the "missing" note of the first whole-tone cycle.[39] The thematic and formal implications of the passage remain dependent upon the context in which it occurs in the given composition, but its immediate *harmonic* meaning may be described entirely apart from this context in terms of the symmetrical partitioning of the tone material into the two whole-tone collections. An economical way of describing that meaning would be to say that the given passage is "in the whole-tone trope" (ex. 69).

EXAMPLE 69

39. The new thematic idea in the following bar is registrally bounded by *e♭* and *c♯*. Perhaps it is not supererogatory to point out that these are the "missing" notes of the second whole-tone cycle.

The "immediate reference" of example 68 is exactly the same as that of the following passage from Berg's *Wozzeck*, and of countless other passages in post-tonal music (ex. 70).

EXAMPLE 70

Copyright 1926, renewed 1954 by Universal Edition, A.G., Vienna.
Used by permission.

In examples 68 and 70 the harmonic content is totally determined by the whole-tone trope. More frequently a whole-tone segment serves to set apart a melodic or harmonic detail from other components that are not thus characterized. In *Wozzeck*, for example, a number of important motives, consisting, like bars 9–10 of Opus 11, No. 1, of hexachordal collections comprising a five-note whole-tone segment plus one "odd" note, occur in combination with motives and simultaneities that are not characterized by whole-tone elements.[40]

The principal figure of Berg's Quartet, Opus 3, is such a collection (ex. 71,a). The opening bars may be entirely analyzed in terms of different interval cycles. The semitonal adjacency that results from the interpolation of an "odd" note in the whole-tone cycle is symmetrically expanded (ex. 71,b) along diverging semitones. The final note of the headmotif divides the octave ambitus of bars 1–2 into two tritones, each of which is itself evenly partitioned, by whole steps and "minor thirds" respectively. The "minor third" in viola and cello introduces a second thematic idea (ex. 71,c), formed by aligning segments of descending semitonal and "perfect fourth" cycles. The symmetrical inflections (ex. 71,d) outlining segments of inversionally complementary semitonal cycles are a prolongation of the second thematic idea (ex. 71,c). In bar 5 the initial figure is transposed to the "major sixth" below, an interval which contains an odd number of semitones and which therefore transfers that figure from the whole-tone cycle represented in its initial pitch level to the second of the two whole-tone cycles into which the twelve pitch classes can be partitioned. This second whole-tone collection is completed by the

40. Perle, "The Musical Language of *Wozzeck*," *The Music Forum* (Columbia University Press), I (1967), pp. 240ff.

sustained bb in the second violin and confirmed in the sustained $f\sharp$ in the cello. The first whole-tone area returns in the following bars, but $f\sharp$ remains as a "dissonant" pedal, resolving in bar 7 to $f\natural$, the one note still required to complete the primary whole-tone collection after the entrance of the first violin in bar 7. In bar 9 all the voices except the cello again move into the second whole-tone collection, complete but for ab, which the cello provides on the following downbeat.

EXAMPLE 71

Copyright 1925 by Universal Edition, A.G., Vienna.
Used by permission.

Other examples of the use of interval cycles and strict inversional complementation in Opus 3 have been discussed above (pp. 12f., 77ff.). These procedures may be explained in general compositional terms, but they are still far from providing Opus 3 with a "structure," if that term is taken to mean anything analogous to what we mean by "tonal structure" in reference to music in the major-minor system. The only extended passage in which *every* note can be referred to the unfolding of one or another interval cycle is example 71, but even within this limited context it seems to me an exaggeration to use the term "structure" to imply such an analogy. The partitioning of musical space into two whole-tone collections organizes pitches in one way, the alignment of complementary cycles at sum 11 (b) and at sum 1 (d) organizes pitches in other ways. Obviously, these pitch structures are compositionally interrelated, but this relationship depends on "reflexive reference," that is, thematic associations uniquely characteristic of the given work, even though their immediate harmonic meaning is not reflexive. In the course of this study we have shown that the collections of sum-11 and sum-1 dyads and the two whole-tone partitions may be viewed as integral components of an overall precompositionally definable system, but such a system does not yet govern the quartet nor any other of the works which we commonly call "atonal."

The symmetrical tetrachord which was labelled "cell z" in our discussion of the first movement of Bartók's Fourth Quartet (p. 10, above) plays an important structural role as the chief non-reflexive component of the fourth of Webern's Five Movements for String Quartet, Opus 5. It appears at four transpositional levels which intersect through common dyads to form the series of tritones illustrated in example 72. Exactly the same relation between successive transpositions of the same cell (ex. 73) plays an important role in the second movement of Bartók's Second Quartet. The movement opens with a signal figure that outlines the principal pitch level of the cell. Overlapping statements lead to a continually reiterated d, the latter being part of an incomplete statement (a-$e\flat$-d) whose close is found in a melodic figure outlined by the tritone d-$g\sharp$.

EXAMPLE 72

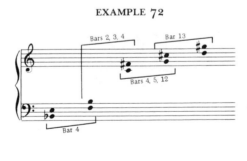

EXAMPLE 73

The two compositions are as unlike one another stylistically as they could possibly be, but the immediate harmonic meaning of the overlapping statements of the cell is exactly the same in both.

The structural function of cell z is inherent. The interval couple of two tritones eliminates tritone transpositions as independent forms, since the tritone is its own T(6) transposition. Any given transposition of the cell will intersect with any other transposition through a shared tritone, or not at all. Successive intersecting transpositions will generate a progression that may be interpreted as unfolding along an interval-7 (or 5) cycle, as in example 72, or an interval-1 (or 11) cycle, as in example 74.

EXAMPLE 74

Successive transpositions by interval-2 (or 10) generate the twelve-tone trope illustrated in example 1 and are equivalent to successive transpositions by interval-8 (or 4). Successive transpositions by interval-3 (or 9) are symmetrically related, sharing either of two axes of symmetry separated by the "minor third" as explained in our earlier discussion of Bartók's Fourth Quartet (pp. 11f.). Whatever we choose to do with cell z, its structural implications are impossible to evade. There are only two other independent tetrachords that contain an interval couple of two tritones, and the properties of these are exactly analogous to those of cell z. They are well known to the traditional tonal system as the "diminished seventh" and "French sixth" chords. Cell z plays no role in the traditional system, and this may explain the special role assigned to it by post-tonal composers.

One of Berg's last tonal works, the second song of Opus 2, opens with a series of "French sixth" chords that may be interpreted, like the above series of cell z tetrachords (examples 72 and 74), as an interval-1 or interval-7 progression (ex. 75).

EXAMPLE 75

Both cycles are simultaneously projected in the composition, in the relation between the outer voices (ex. 76). This equivalence of the two cycles in respect to transpositions of the "French sixth" explains much more about the harmonic language of the piece than does its key signature of six flats.

EXAMPLE 76

If, in the preceding paragraphs, we have chosen to discuss Opus 11, No. 1, rather than Opus 11, No. 3, and one of Webern's Five Movements rather than one of the Six Bagatelles for String Quartet, it is because we are here concerned with those elements in atonal music that are an exception to the principle of "reflexive reference." For any given atonal composition, the relation between the normative and the reflexive, between what can be explained in precompositional terms and what can only be explained contextually, is ultimately imponderable. It is nevertheless clear that some atonal compositions come much closer than others in conforming to "the extreme statement of an ideal condition" implied by the term "reflexive reference." It was Schoenberg's hope that his twelve-tone system would enlarge the domain of the normative component of atonal music, by laying "the foundations for a new procedure in musical construction to replace those structural differentiations provided formerly by tonal harmonies."[41] In itself, the mere presence of a tone row from which every element in a composition is presumably derived does not achieve this aim. On the contrary, at first sight it seems to put the principle of "reflexive reference" on a more secure footing: if "the primary reference of any [note-group] is to something inside the [composition] itself," that "something" has now become a delimited, identifiable, concrete, and exclusive entity. In point of fact, the tone row both enlarges and diminishes the relevance of "reflexive reference" to post-tonal music.

Consider the pitch-class collection 11 10 9 5, listed as No. 19i under "Four-Note Collections" in the Appendix to *Serial Composition and Atonality*. The information given to us there respecting this collection is entirely negative. Unlike Four-Note Collections Nos. 1 through 15, it is *not* self-invertible. Unlike Four-Note Collections Nos. 1, 2, and 7, it is *not*

41. Schoenberg, *op. cit.*, p. 218.

self-transposable. Unlike Nos. 1–6 and 16, it will *not* partition the twelve
pitch classes into transpositionally related segments. Thus it has none of
the properties that characterize the non-reflexive components of atonal
music discussed above. We can take note of certain hypothetical associations with these non-reflexive components—the tritone, a three-note segment of the semitonal scale, a three-note constituent of one of the two
whole-tone collections—but in the absence of a context the given tetrachord derives no meaning from these. The following twelve-tone row
commences with an ordered version of the same four notes:

$$\overline{10 \quad 9 \quad 5 \quad 11} \quad 0 \quad 7 \quad 1 \quad 6 \quad 8 \quad 2 \quad 3 \quad 4$$

If we hypothesize a hexachordal segmentation of this row, we will find
that the content of each hexachord is duplicated in the content of the
non-corresponding hexachord of an inverted form of the same row com-
mencing at the "perfect fifth" below, as in Schoenberg's "combinatorial"
pieces:

$$P_{10}: \quad 10 \quad 9 \quad 5 \quad 11 \quad 0 \quad 7 \; / \; 1 \quad 6 \quad 8 \quad 2 \quad 3 \quad 4$$

$$I_3: \quad 3 \quad 4 \quad 8 \quad 2 \quad 1 \quad 6 \; / \; 0 \quad 7 \quad 5 \quad 11 \quad 10 \quad 9$$

If we hypothesize a tetrachordal segmentation, we will find that the content of each segment is duplicated between corresponding segments of
P_{10} and the retrograde form of the same I set, as in the example from
Webern (ex. 7):

$$P_{10}: \quad 10 \quad 9 \quad 5 \quad 11 \; / \; 0 \quad 7 \quad 1 \quad 6 \; / \; 8 \quad 2 \quad 3 \quad 4$$

$$RI_3: \quad 9 \quad 10 \quad 11 \quad 5 \; / \; 7 \quad 0 \quad 6 \quad 1 \; / \; 2 \quad 8 \quad 4 \quad 3$$

None of the above hypotheses is relevant to the compositional exploitation of the given tetrachord as a segment of this twelve-tone row in the
third movement of Berg's *Lyric Suite*. Two referential components are
derived from the row. One of these is the above-mentioned tetrachordal
collection, which is embedded in the principal set form (ex. 77) at T(0),

$$11 \quad 10 \quad 9 \quad 5$$

T(2),

$$1 \quad 0 \quad 11 \quad 7$$

T(5),

$$4 \quad 3 \quad 2 \quad 10$$

and sum-of-complementation 1,

$$2 \quad 3 \quad 4 \quad 8$$

EXAMPLE 77

Each of these instances of the given tetrachord is represented at T(0) in a different form of the set (ex. 78).

EXAMPLE 78

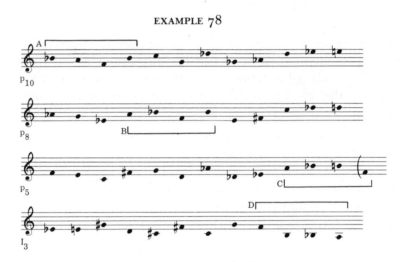

P_8, P_5, and I_3, while preserving the contour assigned to the principal set form, are cyclically permuted so that each commences with the same tetrachordal collection, marked by brackets in the example. This "pattern of internal references" is explicable only "in terms of the principle of reflexive reference," though it is ordered and controlled to a degree that has no precedent in the music of "free" atonality.

The second referential component derived from the row is non-reflexive—explicit compositional statements of seven-note segments of the semitonal scale, implied in the registral distribution of pitches in the principal set form (ex. 79).

EXAMPLE 79

This cyclic component, however, is only an incidental feature of the row, projected by means of a special compositional procedure, rather than a structural property that establishes systematic precompositional relations among the different set forms.

Such systematic precompositional relations depend on precisely the same features that characterize non-reflexive components in "free" atonal music. The difference is that in the twelve-tone system these components are defined as segments of a twelve-tone set.

The concept of the interval cycle as a means of symmetrically partitioning the tone material emerges concomitantly with the weakening and eventual elimination of traditional harmonic functions in post-tonal music and the replacement of a diatonic scale of unequal degrees by an undifferentiated semitonal scale. In the music of Liszt, Wagner, Rimsky-Korsakoff, and other composers of the nineteenth century, one often finds tonal progressions that "modulate" or move sequentially through a series of whole-steps, minor thirds, major thirds, or even tritones. The following passage from Chopin's Prelude in E♭ (ex. 80) aligns a descending interval-1 and an ascending interval-2 cycle in terms of the common pitch-class content of T(1) and T(10) transpositions of the diminished seventh chord.[42] The progression is determined by inherent "extra-tonal" properties of the diminished seventh chord, just as the analogous progression in Berg's Opus 2 (exx. 75–76) is determined by the corresponding properties of the "French sixth" chord.

EXAMPLE 80

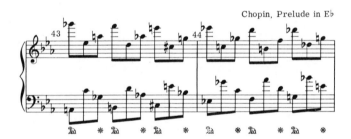

Chopin, Prelude in E♭

The striking juxtaposition of non-symmetrical and cyclically-derived symmetrical formations in Stravinsky's *Sacre* are discussed in my article, cited above (p. 76). The early years of the present century bring us, in consequence of the disappearance of conventional normative elements in the atonal music of Schoenberg and his school, to "an ultimate expansion of possible relations to include the whole range of combinations contained in the semitonal scale."[43] We have shown how the convergence of the concepts of the interval cycle and (through the twelve-tone system) of strict inversional complementation leads to a comprehensive *system* of tone relations that permits us to define and classify every one of these

42. I am indebted to Mark DeVoto for calling my attention to this passage.
43. Perle, *Serial Composition and Atonality*, p. 1.

combinations in terms of its sums and intervals, and consequently to establish differentiations, associations, and progressions between and among all these combinations.

Their sum and interval content are the sole objective basis for whatever connections one may wish to establish between pitch collections, and what else is it to "compose" except to establish such connections? Schoenberg's use of the "augmented triad" in Opus 11, No. 1, and Opus 46;[44] Webern's use of symmetrical tetrachords as basic cells in Opus 5, No. 4;[45] the symmetrical formations in the works of Bartók and Berg; the whole-tone collections in *Wozzeck;* invariant set segments in the later works of Scriabin[46] and in the mature twelve-tone works of Schoenberg, Berg, and Webern; Webern's use of "cognate" sets in the Symphony and elsewhere, and his use of consistent complementary relations among set forms in the Symphony and Saxophone Quartet—the structural functions of all of these are explicable only in terms of sum and interval content and ordering. They may be objectively defined, generalized, and integrated with one another. Collectively they imply a natural system of twelve-tone tonality.

44. *Ibid.,* pp. 14f. and 93.
45. *Ibid.,* pp. 16ff.
46. *Ibid.,* pp. 41ff.

Index
to Basic Definitions

Index
to Compositions

3 1543 50111 5309

781.61
P451t

790816

DATE DUE

JE 22'81			

Cressman Library
Cedar Crest College
Allentown, Pa. 18104

DEMCO